A Parent's Survival Guide to Common Core Math

Grades K-5

Christen Nine, M.Ed.
Mathematics Educator
Founder of Mathstream.TV

Mathstream.TV
PO Box 4073
Manchester, NH 03108
www.mathstream.tv

Cover Photo © Dollarphotoclub.com, purchased with appropriate permissions.

To email the author directly, send to:
Mrs9@mathstream.tv

Dedication

This book is dedicated, first, to my husband for his ceaseless encouragement and help in making this idea a reality, and secondly, to our two young children for sacrificing many hours and bedtime stories for the sake of this finished product.

Special thanks to my parents, Timothy and Susan Byrd, and my long-time colleague and friend, Amy Gentile, for their late night sessions of commenting, editing, and questioning, trying to make this the best resource possible. And many thanks to the countless educators, colleagues, and students who have imparted the insight necessary to write this book.

Table of Contents

Table of Contents

Introduction 7

Chapter 1 **The Standards for Mathematical Practice**......................11

Chapter 2 **The Common Core State Standards for Mathematics**.....19

Chapter 3 **Building Number Recognition and Intuition**.................33

Chapter 4 **Understanding Place Value**..45

Chapter 5 **Addition and Subtraction**..61

Chapter 6 **Statistics Foundation (Organizing Data)**....................103

Chapter 7 **Multiplication and Division**..113

Chapter 8 **Fractions**..139

Chapter 9 **Decimal Numbers**...165

In Closing **Conceptual Understanding is Key**..............................175

About the Author...177

References 179

Glossary..181

Introduction

It is no secret among education professionals that the face of U.S. education is constantly changing. Whether it be the pendulum swing of how to teach reading (Phonics? Whole word learning? No, definitely phonics!) or the development of new areas of education like Special Ed, the one thing that a seasoned college professor will be able to confidently tell his or her teachers-in-training is that nothing is here to stay. Does that mean that we as a nation should ignore the constant attempts to alter the methodology and economics of our education structure? Tempting as this may sound, to do so would be to miss out on maximizing the effectiveness of bringing the *current* theories to our *current* generation of students in the best ways we know how.

What is the "big talk" of the 2010 decade of education? We probably have all heard about it by now: "Common Core" – the great education game changer. Will it be here to stay? Probably not in its current form. Just like any educational shift, it will become a foundation for future ideas, or we will react to it in disapproval by swinging that pendulum of educational theory in the opposite direction—or perhaps, we will do a little of both. But one thing is certain, this generation of students will be greatly influenced by the standards and expectations set forth by this newest development of the educational metamorphosis.

Common Core is a complicated educational initiative, presenting different questions and concerns for each area of study, as well as big picture questions regarding Standardized Testing and Political Motivation. I would be crazy to think that I could address or answer all of these questions. My area of expertise is mathematics education: both for the traditional and the learning disabled student. My undergraduate and graduate studies, combined with my years of teaching, convince me that mathematics education has the potential to be better in the next century than it has been in the one that is behind us. We are learning more and more about how students succeed and struggle; we are undertaking research endeavors to understand how the brain processes new knowledge; and we are gaining the courage to set aside our age-old, familiar teaching methods for the sake of educational training that is clearly backed and supported by current research.

This all sounds inspirational on paper, but we have to ask ourselves: Is it possible to turn a ship as great and complex as a whole nation's education methods? Can you implement one new education initiative, like the Common Core Standards for Mathematics, and instantaneously turn students, teachers, and parents on to the idea of a new progression and new methods of teaching a subject as age-old as mathematics? How can teachers "grandfather" students caught in the middle of the shift when no time is allowed to slowly transition to the new order of learning? How can parents help their students with mathematics homework when the methods are unfamiliar?

These are the problems that schools and parents are currently encountering with their students, especially in the elementary grades, where teaching foundational math concepts is critical and where the expectation that parents are able to be "at home" tutors is often taken for granted. This book is an attempt to pull together some introductory information that will help parents of students, grades K-5, feel more empowered to provide the elementary math help that they wish to offer. This book is not an attempt to debate the pros and cons of the Common Core Standards. That is material for quite a different book. However, I hope that what you will find in this book will be both practical and useful to *surviving* this huge educational transition which, if nothing else, is certainly here for *this* generation of students.

Christen Nine
Author of "A Parent's Survival Guide to Common Core Math"
Founder of Mathstream.TV

For more information on all topics covered in this book, please check out the electronic resources we have available on our websites:
www.commoncoremath101.com *and*
www.mathstream.tv.

Chapter 1

The Standards for Mathematical Practice

The Common Core State Standards for Mathematics – what exactly are they, anyway? Everyone seems to be attempting to understand the answer to that question: teachers, students, and parents alike. Some people feel that the Common Core State Standards are making mathematics more convoluted and complicated. Others complain that following this new set of Standards will dumb down our students' education. Still others see the standards as a great breakthrough in finally strengthening the quality of math teaching in the United States. While much could be said regarding the political pros and cons of a "Common Core Standard" for Math and English education, the purpose of this book is to bring clarity and confidence to parents regarding the math content and educational practices of mathematics teachers that are being encouraged by the Common Core Standards. Regardless of political leaning or personal opinions, the Common Core State Standards for Mathematics (CCSS-M) are defining the education of millions of U.S. students, and the goal of this book is to help parents feel empowered to understand the material and advocate for their students' education in the ways they ought to be able to.

Before we consider the standards themselves, it is vital that we consider the big picture of what these standards are attempting to accomplish. The Common Core State Standards Initiative (2015d) summarized their grand vision into eight phrases which they have called the "Standards for Mathematical Practice" (SMP); they are listed below as direct quotes from the CCSS Initiative's website and are summarized in practical, layman's terms:

"Make sense of problems and persevere in solving them."

The first SMP states that a quality teacher of mathematics will train their students in two specific ways: first, to be able to independently decode mathematical questions into something they can make sense of, and secondly, to have the confidence and persistence to solve and answer those questions. While this may sound like an obvious goal, consider that prior mathematics education standards and practices have frequently emphasized memorization and regurgitation techniques instead of sense-making techniques. This has often left students with a head full of memorized facts but limited ability to solve novel math problems that do not fit the cookie cutter presentation they received in the classroom.

"Reason abstractly and quantitatively."
Mathematics problem-solving utilizes both abstract (big picture) and quantitative (specific detail) reasoning. A student needs to be trained to pull themselves back from a math problem and decide what kind of mathematical situation they are actually addressing. In a sense, math teachers are responsible for teaching their students to SEE the Forest for the Trees, to be able to decide if they are looking at an addition, multiplication, volume, or statistics problem on their own without being specifically told in the directions. Useful math skills should be extendable to the real world, not just a math test. In the real world, the mathematician (aka, any average person solving a math problem) needs to decide the type of problem they are addressing independent of any instructions. Additionally, on the quantitative end of the math solving spectrum, students need to be able to look at the specific details of a math problem and be able to assign appropriate values, variables, and meaning to the minutia of the situation. A big picture approach to math will only get you started. Attention to quantitative detail is critical in finding a math solution.

"Construct viable arguments and critique the reasoning of others."

During my years as a high school mathematics teacher, I had the rare privilege of teaching my favorite math class as a first year teacher: Calculus. Fresh out of college and eager to give my students meaningful math experiences, a colleague and I were able to take the Calculus class to a local engineering company to see the ins and outs of life in the engineering working world. During our tour of the facilities, one of the guides singled me out as the teacher, and said essentially, "If you are a good teacher, you will make sure that your students can do more than just solve math problems. You need to teach them to communicate their solution to others. If you send me the most brilliant mathematician in the world to work on my team, I won't care unless they know how to explain their solutions to other people." I took his words to heart and have remembered them as I have continued in my teaching career. When I first read this third SMP, I harkened back to that intense moment with the Engineer tour guide. A good math teacher will train their student to communicate effectively with other students (or in a greater sense, with other Mathematicians). This skill in communication and collaboration is important for formulating and reformulating one's own math reasoning as well as the reasoning of others.

"Model with mathematics."

Mathematical Modeling is the skill that helps a student to translate a real world situation into mathematical language. Equations with variables, addition and subtraction sentences, and geometric pictures are just a few examples of models that could be used to rewrite a situation into mathematical language that can be analyzed and solved. This SMP is foundational in making mathematics applicable and valuable in real life, not just in the classroom.

"Use appropriate tools strategically."
Math tools are the physical objects or resources (technology, hands-on learning materials, etc.) that a student has at their disposal for solving math problems. The simplest combination of math solution tools would be a pencil and some paper, but many more complicated manipulatives, software, measuring tools, and calculators are also available. Teachers of mathematics are being encouraged now, possibly more than ever, to make these resources available to students and to guide them in learning how and when to make use of them.

"Attend to precision."
This SMP may strike some readers as surprising, since there has been pervasive miscommunication in the media and on various blog sites regarding this aspect of the Common Core State Standards for Mathematics. Many people have been under the impression that the "New Math" of the Common Core promotes a "there are no wrong answers" attitude. Hopefully the emphasis placed on *precision* will encourage those who have worried about these rumors. The CCSS-M clearly state that, at every educational level, one of the eight most important math

skills taught in the classroom should be precision: clear communication of variables and measurements, appropriate use of math symbolism, and of course, correct answers. During my time as a high school math teacher, I liked to remind my students that, in the real world of business, engineering, budgeting, bill payments, accounting, mortgages, tax payments, and the like, people only care about two things when it comes to real-world mathematics: efficiency and accuracy. At the end of the day, these are the lasting qualities we hope to instill in our math students for future use, and this is emphasized especially clearly in this sixth Standard for Math Practice.

"Look for and make use of structure."
In many ways, mathematics is really a study of numeric patterns. From the simplest of math operations and shapes learned in Kindergarten to the most complicated derivatives discussed in High School Calculus, mathematics is an expression of beautiful and predictable patterns, some more obvious than others. In past decades of math teaching, these patterns were hardly mentioned, probably because they seemed too obvious to the especially brilliant math minds and too irrelevant to the average teacher. In fact, this concept is probably the one that has created the most controversy over the CCSS-M. Is it a waste of time to make "pattern" studying a cornerstone of math education? As someone who has made mathematics and education my focus of study, I would earnestly say—*absolutely not*; it is a brilliant and significant use of time as a math educator! A student who can discover and understand the patterns involved in addition, subtraction, multiplication, division,

fractions, and the multitude of other topics studied from Kindergarten through High School, will become a student who is able to quickly catch their own errors when solving mathematics problems. The students who perform best in math classrooms are the ones who can find their errors before the teacher does (and before the teacher grades their test!). In past decades, we have erroneously labeled these students as "good at math" and the others as "just not good at math". I did an informal survey recently of 100 individuals' reaction to "math" as either favorable or unfavorable; the split turned out to be roughly 50/50. Consistently, I heard people respond to my question by saying something like, "I just always got math, so I would say that it is favorable," or conversely, "I just was always bad at math. I don't get math, so I find it unfavorable." The roughly 50% of people who "get math" are the ones who see the patterns almost without effort. In past years, we have left the other half of our students to flounder and eventually to simply celebrate high school graduation as the day when they can leave that "stupid math" behind them forever. However, we are now realizing that it is possible to actually teach students to look for, to see, and to make use of the patterns found throughout mathematics IF the teacher uses EXPLICIT (clear and forthright) teaching strategies in the earliest years to develop this skill. There will always be the 50% of students who can find these patterns without help, but we no longer believe, as mathematics educators, that this is reason enough to leave the other 50% behind. Many of the "New Math" techniques (which are truthfully just "Newer Methods") mentioned in the following chapters are related to this second-to-last, and especially important, Standard for Mathematical Practice.

"Look for and express regularity in repeated reasoning."

The ability to find patterns in mathematics, as described in the previous SMP, will also allow students to find patterns, or repetitions, in how they can best solve problems. This ability to know when and how to use the same (or different) problem solving methods can only be done effectively if students really understand the *why* behind the mathematics. As a high school math teacher, I remember how frequently my students, as well as the students of colleagues, struggled to remember how to multiply fractions. They would interchange the algorithms for proportions and fraction multiplication without realizing, and the result would be wildly erroneous answers. The students could not remember which algorithm to use because they did not understand why those algorithms even worked to begin with. Instead of being taught to understand fraction operations in the primary grades, they had been taught simply how to perform a list of steps without meaning. Years later, they still could not remember which procedure to use at the appropriate time. Under the SMP for the Common Core, teachers are finally being asked to place special emphasis on training students to be able to use repeated reasoning at the appropriate time. The foundation of this practice is teaching for understanding *and* mastery, not trusting rote memorization to be sufficient instruction.

Chapter 2

The Common Core State Standards for Mathematics

Now that we have considered the eight Standards for Mathematical Practice, we are ready to discuss the content and the educational implications of the Common Core State Standards for Mathematics (CCSS-M). (Note that we are now talking about the Grade Level Standards for Mathematics, not just the Standards for Mathematical Practice discussed in Chapter 1.)

It is of primary importance that we first clarify that nothing about the Standards is a "Curriculum". This means that the Standards themselves do not include a list of homework problems and assignments that your child must complete before graduation. There are no required math textbooks. In fact, at the writing of this book, the textbook companies are still scrambling to decide exactly how to rewrite their old materials. Many resources have enthusiastic claims about being "Common Core Aligned", but sadly, this is no guarantee that the materials within those books are a quality interpretation of the standards. Since the CCSS-M has put extra emphasis on developing both understanding *and* mastery, and because prior math pedagogy often left *understanding* to the 50% who simply "got it" (see Chapter 1 under heading: "Look for and make use of structure.") and never bothered instructing the struggling *other* half to overcome that comprehension gap, many of the textbook companies themselves do not know how to rewrite the math correctly. A quick internet search of "Bad Common Core Math Problems" should make the blundering of the curriculum companies quite apparent. However, it is important to remember that these problems were created by textbook companies or teachers; they are not included in (or even part of) the actual Common Core State Standards.

So, if the Standards are NOT a Curriculum, then what are they? The Standards are really a list of expectations that guide teachers about what students need to master at each grade level. For Kindergarten through Grade 8, teachers are given 3 or 4 big ideas (only 2 for Kindergarten) called "Critical Area" to focus on per grade (Common Core State Standards Initiative, 2015b). These 3 or 4 areas are further detailed in roughly 10 specific items, organized into categories called domains. The six learning domains that are addressed in Kindergarten through Grade 5 math are as follows: Counting and Cardinality, Operations and Algebraic Thinking, Number and Operations in Base Ten, Number and Operations—Fractions, Measurement and Data, and Geometry. The following two tables show how the Critical Areas, the Domains, and the most important specific items fit together in the elementary grades. The information is directly quoted from the Common Core State Standards Initiative's website to insure the integrity of the outline (Common Core Standards Initiative, 2015b, see Grade Level Introductions):

Table 1: Kindergarten - Grade 2 Standards Outline

	Kindergarten	**Grade 1**	**Grade 2**
Critical Areas	*1) representing and comparing whole numbers initially with sets of objects* *2) describing shapes and space*	*1) developing understanding of addition, subtraction, and strategies for addition and subtraction within 20* *2) developing understanding of whole number relationships and place value, including grouping in tens and ones* *3) developing understanding of linear measurement and measuring lengths as iterating length units* *4) reasoning about attributes of, and composing and decomposing geometric shapes*	*1) extending understanding of base-ten notation* *2) building fluency with addition and subtraction* *3) using standard units of measure* *4) describing and analyzing shapes*
Counting & Cardinality	- Know number names and the count sequence. - Count to tell the number of objects. - Compare numbers.	N/A	N/A

Operations & Algebraic Thinking	- Understand addition as putting together and adding to, and understand subtraction as taking apart and taking from.	- Represent and solve problems involving addition and subtraction. - Understand and apply properties of operations and the relationship between addition and subtraction. - Add and subtract within 20. -Work with addition and subtraction equations.	- Represent and solve problems involving addition and subtraction. - Add and subtract within 20. -Work with equal groups of objects to gain foundations for multiplication.
Number & Operations in Base 10	- Work with numbers 11-19 to gain foundations for place value.	- Extend the counting sequence. - Understand place value. - Use place value understanding and properties of operations to add and subtract.	- Understand place value. - Use place value understanding and properties of operations to add and subtract.
Measurement & Data	- Describe and compare measurable attributes. - Classify objects and count the number of objects in each category.	- Measure lengths indirectly and by iterating length units. - Tell and write time. - Represent and interpret data.	- Measure and estimate lengths in standard units. - Relate addition and subtraction to length. - Work with time and money. - Represent and interpret data.

Geometry	- Identify and describe shapes. - Analyze, compare, create, and compose shapes.	- Reason with shapes and their attributes.	- Reason with shapes and their attributes.

24

Table 2: Grade 3 - Grade 5 Standards Outline

	Grade 3	Grade 4	Grade 5
Critical Areas	*1) developing understanding of multiplication and division strategies for multiplication and division within 100* *2) developing understanding of fractions, especially unit fractions (fractions with numerator 1)* *3) developing understanding of the structure of rectangular arrays and of area* *4) describing and analyzing two-dimensional shapes*	*1) developing understanding and fluency with multi-digit multiplication, and developing understanding of dividing to find quotients involving multi-digit dividends* *2) developing an understanding of fraction equivalence, addition and subtraction of fractions with like denominators, and multiplication of fractions by whole numbers* *3) understanding that geometric figures can be analyzed and classified based on their properties, such as having parallel sides, perpendicular sides, particular angle measures, and symmetry*	*1) developing fluency with addition and subtraction of fractions, and developing understanding of the multiplication of fractions and division of fractions in limited cases (unit fractions divided by whole numbers and whole numbers divided by unit fractions)* *2) extending division to 2-digit divisors, integrating decimal fractions into the place value system and developing understanding of operations with decimals to hundredths, and developing, and developing fluency with whole number and decimal operations* *3) developing understanding of volume*

Operations & Algebraic Thinking	- Represent and solve problems involving multiplication and division. - Understand properties of multiplication and the relationship between multiplication and division. - Multiply and divide within 100. - Solve problems involving the four operations, and identify and explain patterns in arithmetic.	- Use the four operations with whole numbers to solve problems. - Gain familiarity with factors and multiples. - Generate and analyze patterns.	- Write and interpret numerical expressions. - Analyze patterns and relationships.
Number & Operations in Base 10	- Use place value understanding and properties of operations to perform multi-digit arithmetic.	- Generalize place value understanding for multi-digit whole numbers. - Use place value understanding and properties of operations to perform multi-digit arithmetic.	- Understand the place value system. - Perform operations with multi-digit whole numbers and with decimals to hundredths.

26

Number & Operations -- Fractions	- Develop understanding of fractions as numbers.	- Extend understanding of fraction equivalence and ordering. - Build fractions from unit fractions by applying and extending previous understandings of operations on whole numbers. - Understand decimal notation for fractions, and compare decimal fractions.	- Use equivalent fractions as a strategy to add and subtract fractions. - Apply and extend previous understandings of multiplication and division to multiply and divide fractions.
Measurement & Data	- Solve problems involving measurement and estimation of intervals of time, liquid volumes, and masses of objects. - Represent and interpret data. - Geometric measurement: understand concepts of area and relate area to multiplication and addition. - Geometric measurement: recognize perimeter as an attribute of plane figures and distinguish between linear and area measures.	- Solve problems involving measurement and conversion of measurements from a larger unit to a smaller unit. - Represent and interpret data. - Geometric measurement: understand concepts of angle and measure angles.	- Convert like measurement units within a given measurement system. - Represent and interpret data. - Geometric measurement: understand concepts of volume and relate volume to multiplication and to addition.

Geometry	- Reason with shapes and their attributes.	- Draw and identify lines and angles, and classify shapes by properties of their lines and angles.	- Graph points on the coordinate plane to solve real-world and mathematical problems. - Classify two-dimensional figures into categories based on their properties.

If these charts seem a bit lacking in detail, you are not mistaken. This is just the bare-bones version of the Standards, highlighting the overarching goals for each grade. Each of the roughly 10 items listed per grade level are further detailed by a handful of more specific explanations which are given highly technical codes like: "CCSS.Math.Content.1.OA.A.2". This particular code is shorthand for: Math Content for Grade 1, Expectation for "Operations & Algebraic Thinking", Subcategory A, Standard 2. (What a mouthful.) More specifically, CCSS.Math.Content.1.OA.A.2 states that first graders must, "Solve word problems that call for addition of three whole numbers whose sum is less than or equal to 20, e.g., by using objects, drawings, and equations with a symbol for the unknown number to represent the problem" (Common Core State Standards Initiative, 2015a, para. 2).

If reading hundreds of highly technical phrases like this gives you a headache, take heart, I will spare you. In the chapters that follow, I will only highlight the standards that have caused parents and students confusion with the recent shift to Common Core, and even then, I will write in layman's terms. As I write, keep in mind that each standard is written rather blandly, leaving much open to the teacher's interpretation. Because of this, the examples I use in the following chapters are representative, but not exhaustive examples of the problems appearing in children's homework.

If you would appreciate understanding and reading the more minute details of the Standards, check out the following links to the Common Core State Standards Initiative Website. Each of these links will give you the most detailed breakdown of the grade level expectations in each domain:

Counting and Cardinality:
www.corestandards.org/Math/Content/CC/

Operations and Algebraic Thinking:
www.corestandards.org/Math/Content/OA/

Number and Operations in Base Ten:
www.corestandards.org/Math/Content/NBT/

Number and Operations—Fractions:
www.corestandards.org/Math/Content/NF/

Measurement and Data:
www.corestandards.org/Math/Content/MD/

Geometry:
www.corestandards.org/Math/Content/G/

If you find that you still have unanswered questions about specific homework problems after reading through the examples found in this book, please visit our websites, www.commoncoremath101.com and www.mathstream.tv, to view our additional resources, follow our updates, or send us a message.

Section 1

Challenging and New Material
Grades K-2

Chapter 3

Building Number Recognition and Intuition

In his book *How the Brain Learns Mathematics*, David Sousa (2008) explained a number of studies that were conducted between 1980 and 2006 that investigated the ability of infants to recognize when the number of a group of objects changes. Although infants might seem like an unlikely test group for a study about numbers, the research results did not disappoint. In fact, the studies proved that infants who are *only a few months old* are already able to use their brains to recognize, in a very basic sense, the concepts of *equal groups*, *more and less*, and *two or three*. These cognitive skills have been important for the survival of the human species, since the ability to assess one's environment for advantages and disadvantages (based on quantity) is what has given us the aptitude to decide when "fight or flight" is the appropriate response to danger. Thus, it is not surprising to find that these skills start to develop in a child's brain within the first months of life. As infants mature into young children, this *intuitive* number sense, combined with a basic knowledge of numbers, develops into something that math educators refer to as "subitizing" (Sousa, 2008, p.13). Subitizing is the brain's ability to quickly recognize the actual number of objects in a group without counting. Studies have shown that the human brain can subitize for quantities of one, two, three, or four only. For quantities greater than four, our brains need extra help and structure to be able to recognize the number of objects; either we must count them, or we must use a familiar pattern to make recognition easier. For instance, the

number five is much easier to recognize this way: ,

than this: . However, even with the second image, our brains might quickly notice groupings such as: 1 dot, 2 dots, and 2 dots. If we know basic arithmetic, we can easily sum 1+2+2 to find a total of 5. Thus we find that, while the first image is recognizable immediately as "5", the second image requires a bit more time and math knowledge to interpret. The number of dots in each picture are exactly the same, but the familiar *representation* of the die-face gives our brain a little extra help in identifying the amount.

In short, there are two keys to making number recognition quick and easy. Either you can *present numbers visually in the same manner every time*, or you can *present them in a way that makes grouping and counting easy.* With this in mind, educators have begun utilizing a memorization tool called a **Ten Frame** to help students be able to quickly recognize whole numbers 0 through 10. You will note in the following examples that, contrary to the faces of a die, a Ten Frame has flexibility to represent numbers in a variety of ways. However, the basic structure of the Frame limits these variations to something a Kindergartener can still easily connect to and recognize.

An empty **Ten Frame** looks quite simply like this:

We can represent *any* whole number from zero to ten using this model. As an Example, let's consider Eight, which could be represented like this:

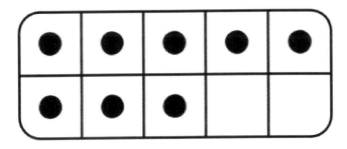

...or this...

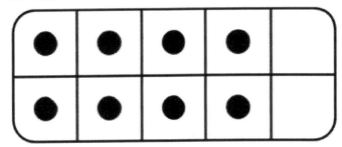

...or even this...

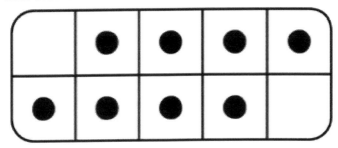

This visual tool helps students to practice *seeing* the quantity "eight" in its various formations, each one a meaningful picture of its value: as *5 and 3*, as *4 and 4*, and even as *2 less than 10*.

This last reference to the benchmark of *ten* is intentional, since our Place Value System requires us to think continually about numbers in groups of ten. Ten Frames are an excellent tool for introducing this most basic Place Value skill, something we call **Making 10**. For instance, if given the symbolic number "8" or even the Ten Frame , students need to become fluent in being able to identify the number that would bring their current number to 10. In this case, "2" is the number that would "Make 10". Thus, we find that visual tools like the Ten Frame help students to see both the *present* quantity as well as the *missing* quantity as they develop their intuitive sense of numbers and basic Base-Ten Place Value skills.

Another visual strategy for giving concrete meaning to numbers is the organizational technique called making **Arrays**. An Array is a rectangular grid of dots or objects that, like Ten Frames, help students to visualize number quantities in more flexible ways. For instance, the number twelve can be displayed as any of the following Arrays:

●●●●●●
●●●●●●

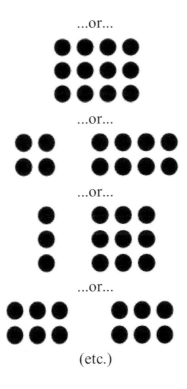

...or...

...or...

...or...

(etc.)

In the lower three examples, we see that the addition facts 4+8=12, 3+9=12, and 6+6=12 are all visually suggested. Often times, students will be given Arrays like the first two examples and will be asked to **Partition** the group in any way that they would like using a line (essentially forming groups like the final three examples on their own). As they learn basic addition facts, they can then use their **Partitioned Arrays** to write a number sentence that fits their model. Consider the following Sample Problem:

<u>Example 1</u>
Partition the following Array in two different ways,
and then write the corresponding addition sentences for
each.

<u>Possible Answer for Example 1</u>

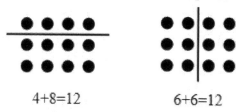

$$4+8=12 \qquad\qquad 6+6=12$$

While Ten Frames and Arrays help students to see numbers
as quantities, a more common, but equally important way
of visualizing numbers is their relative position and value
compared to other numbers on a **Number Line**. This age
old technique for number representation prepares students
to see numbers as having a more continuous relationship.
This is something that will help them transition to
understanding negative and fractional values in later
grades.

Number Lines can be rigidly organized with "dashes" to
indicate regular intervals, or they can be constructed with a
more "open" format with only a few important numbers
shown in relatively appropriate positions. Younger students
require more structure than older students, so Open

Number Lines should not be introduced until Dashed Number Lines have been mastered.

Dashed Number Line:

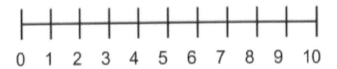

Open Number Line:

Summary

In summary, young children are born with a very basic number sense that teachers and parents can help build upon and develop. Three important tools for bringing tangible meaning to numbers are: Ten Frames, Arrays of Objects, and Number Lines. Ten Frames help students to visualize numbers with a semi-predictable structure that *uses the benchmark of ten* to represent quantities. Arrays allow numbers to be represented as *quantities that can be partitioned* into groups of smaller numbers. Number Lines give meaning to numbers by displaying them *in relation to other values* along a continuum. For early grades, a Dashed Number Line should be used to make the continuum very clear and concrete. Open Number Lines should only be used with upper elementary students.

Parents' main areas of confusion or frustration with this material are related to the new language (such as "Ten Frame", "Making Ten", or "Arrays of Objects"). Additionally, while it is expected that young students will draw pictures or play with blocks occasionally in school, there can often be misunderstanding about the value of math tasks that involve equally as many pictures as numbers (consider Arrays as an example). The purpose of this chapter is to clarify both the terminology and the value in these exercises to promote good number sense in K-2 students.

Just like any teaching tools, the examples described in this chapter will be more or less effective depending on how they are utilized. Consider these three suggestions of how to be a well-informed advocate for quality teaching of number sense:

1. Validate experimentation and play with numbers. Remember that your child's brain is already an amazing resource for basic number intuition. Partner with their teacher to develop this number sense by allowing your child to work with number pictures, to play with manipulatives, or to play math games assigned by the teacher (or from your own research). In order for knowledge to be incorporated in an intuitive manner, students must experiment with that knowledge in a way that feels natural

instead of forced. This does *not* mean that *every* assignment should be games and fun. It simply means that there is a deeper motive behind these activities than meets the eye.

2. Help your student build number sense by maintaining a good balance of visual and symbolic representations. Picture representations and hands-on work is important in math class, but these activities should always lead to a more solid understanding of symbolic mathematics. If you notice an abundance of assignments that have pictorial math but lack symbolic representations of numbers, you can help your student by prompting them to record their answers as both images *and* numbers. For example, if a worksheet asks students to simply partition a handful of Arrays, but does not ask them to represent their answers as actual numbers (symbolic form), you can help your student answer the questions in *both* ways: visually with partitions and symbolically as an addition sentence.

Example: Partition the Array into Three Groups.
(**Note the absence of a Symbolic comparison in this question.)

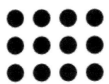

Directions Imply the Following Possible Solution:

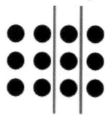

*Parent Could Also Prompt Student for this **Additional***
Answer:
6+3+3 is 12 (*or* 6+3+3=12)

It is important in education (except in obvious, truly negative situations) to give teachers the benefit of the doubt in their choice of activities. They are trained to see the big picture and to introduce activities that will lead students to the desired end-goal of learning and understanding mathematics. However, it is also understandable that parents want to feel that they can express concern when learning does not seem to be progressing as anticipated. This suggestion of how to keep an eye on students' balance and connection between pictorial and symbolic activities is a nice way to validate the homework assignment, as given, while adding an extra step that can only help your child become more proficient in their understanding of numbers. It allows both you and the teacher to maintain an appropriate sense of autonomy in your child's learning process.

3. Help young students practice their numbers by making your own Ten Frame at home. If you take an egg carton with one row removed (to make a 2x5 Frame) and a handful of dried beans, you can help young students practice their number representation and recognition of numbers 0-10. If you make a second 2x5 Frame from another egg carton, they can also represent numbers 11-20. These frames will also become excellent tools for practicing Addition and Subtraction (See Chapter 5: Addition and Subtraction).

For more specific details regarding the Common Core's expectations for development of good number sense from Kindergarten through second grade, see the information provided by the Common Core State Standards Initiative (2015b) on their website under the section heading for "Counting & Cardinality".

See the Math in action!
Check out the companion videos for *Chapter 3* at
www.commoncoremath101.com.

Chapter 4

Understanding Place Value

When I was an early elementary school student, the phrase "place value" would have conjured up images of a large, visually crowded, laminated classroom poster that looked something like this:

Millions	Hundred Thousands	Ten Thousands	Thousands	Hundreds	Tens	Ones	Tenths	Hundreds	Thousandths
1,	0	0	0,	0	0	0 .	0	0	1

While this (very accurate) poster served as a great visual for *seeing* the pattern in place value labeling, it never did much for cultivating an understanding of the Base-Ten number system or for teaching the impact that place value has on all basic math operations. In discussing the way that our brain processes numbers, Sousa (2008) noted that, although the human brain is able to make quick assessments of and comparisons between small, positive numbers, it struggles increasingly to make meaning of larger numbers. Since basic survival skills have required even the earliest humans to pay more attention to the comparison between 90 and 70 than to the difference between 91 and 89 (imagine assessing the threat of enemy invaders as an example), our brains have learned to generalize the information that we receive about larger numbers in our environment. On the contrary, even young children are quick to recognize the distinct difference between the quantities 3 and 4, or between 5 and 6, since the ability to compare small changes in small values is indeed important for survival (consider the need to bring home the appropriate amount of food to feed a family or the ability to consider the odds of success in a fight of three against four). Sousa (2008) further explained the impact of this aspect of our brain functioning on education:

> Students in primary grades have developed a notion of counting but have a difficult time studying subject matter that contains large numbers, such as the population of a country, distances to the planets and stars, and the cost of running a space mission.

Although they are fascinated by large quantities, they have a limited understanding of them and often express exaggerated amounts in their conversation... (Sousa, 2008, p. 109)

Thus, we find that education about large numbers needs to be deliberate and meaningful, allowing students to make connections between their knowledge of small numbers and what they are learning about the meaning of large numbers. Simple memorization of place value labels is indeed important, since the natural ability of the human mind to learn and use language greatly enhances our ability to remember mathematics (Sousa, 2008, p. 44). However, these labels will lack meaning to young students unless they work with tangible representations of large numbers and learn to break apart and compare numbers of various sizes. Without this kind of conceptual understanding, students will lean too heavily on their ability to memorize simple facts and sample problems, a task that often proves difficult and unreliable in the long run.

Present day strategies for teaching Place Value Knowledge starts early, even in Kindergarten, and utilizes a variety of models and representations (Common Core State Standards Initiative, 2015b, Kindergarten: Number & Operations in Base 10 section). One of the most basic of these methods, which is taught in Kindergarten, is the ability to break one number into two smaller parts. This process of breaking a number apart is often referred to as **Decomposing Numbers**. *Note that: Numbers can certainly be decomposed into more than just two parts, but for* *simplicity's sake, we will look at the most basic examples of Number Decomposition first.*

Example 1A
Directions: Find three different ways to Decompose the number 9 into two smaller numbers.

Possible Answer for Example 1A (using a simple **Tree Diagram**)

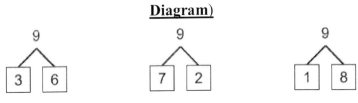

Possible Answer for Example 1A (using a **Tape Diagram**)

9	
3	6

9	
7	2

9	
1	8

Though this exercise does not yet give students any indication of the complexities of Base-Ten Place Value, it does give young children experience in thinking of numbers as quantities that can be broken into parts. Later in Kindergarten, students will also be instructed to Decompose numbers 11 through 19 into groups of 10 and another number. This will be students' first experience relating numbers to groups of 10.

<u>Example 1B</u>

Directions: Decompose the number 13 into ten and ones by completing the following diagram.

13

<u>Answer for Example 1B</u>

13

As students progress in understanding the significance of "tens" in our number system, teachers will likely introduce **Base Ten Blocks**, a not-so-new learning tool that you may possibly recall from your own elementary education experience.

If you don't recall how Base Ten Blocks work, this review should be helpful. First consider the three most commonly used block types.

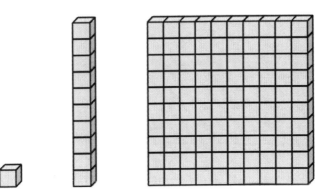

The smallest block in Diagram 1A is called the Unit Block because it represents the quantity "1". I have often heard elementary teachers refer to these small blocks as "Dots" to make it easier for young children to remember. The long thin block is called a Ten Block, or more casually, a "Stick". It is quite literally constructed to be the size of 10 unit blocks. Lastly, the largest block is called a Hundred Block, or simply a "Flat". It is the size of 100 unit blocks, or alternatively, the size of 10 ten blocks. In upper elementary school, students may also consider the Thousand Block, which is a cube the size of 10 hundred blocks (See Diagram 1B below).

Diagram 1B

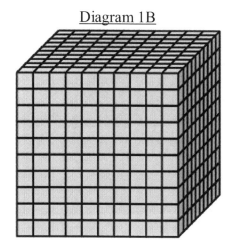

Let us consider a couple of sample questions that K-2
students might be asked to model using **Base Ten Blocks**.

Example 2A
Represent the number 38 with Sticks and Dots,
then record your answer in the boxes below.

Sticks	Dots

Answer to Example 2A
Representation with Blocks

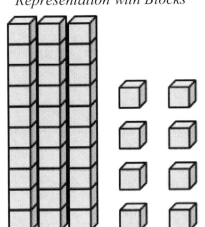

Recorded in Writing

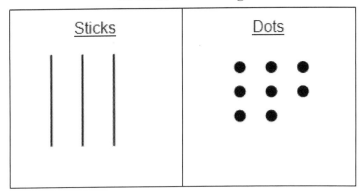

Sticks	Dots

Example 3A

Represent the number 342 with Flats, Sticks and Dots,
then record your answer in the boxes below.

Flats	Sticks	Dots

Answer to Example 3A

Representation with Blocks:

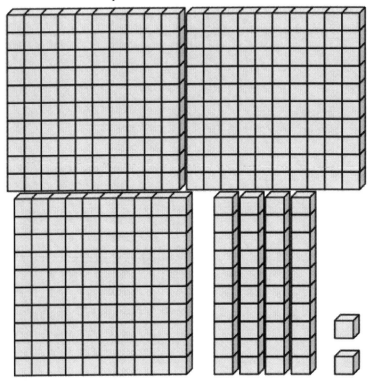

Recorded in Writing:

Flats	Sticks	Dots
□ □ □	| | | |	● ●

After students master simple representations of numbers, these same Base Ten Blocks can be used to bring greater meaning to operations like Addition, Subtraction, Multiplication and Division. (See *Chapter 5: Addition and Subtraction and Chapter 7: Multiplication and Division*)

As students begin to move away from physical models, to more abstract, symbolic representations of numbers, students will be asked to write numbers in **Expanded Form**, which is a natural outflow of the information they have gained from their use of Base Ten Blocks. Consider the following comparisons:

<u>Example 4A</u>
Represent the number 46 as sticks and dots,
explain the groups of blocks that you have,
and then rewrite the number in Expanded Form.

<u>Answer to Example 4A</u>
Representation:

Sticks	Dots
					● ● ● ● ● ●

Groups: 4 tens   6 ones

Expanded Form: 40 + 6 = 46
(After students learn about multiplication, they may also be asked to write this answer as 4*10 + 6*1 = 46.)

Example 4B
Directions: Represent the number 275 with Base Ten Blocks,
explain the number of groups you have,
and rewrite the number in expanded form.

Answer to Example 4B
Representation:

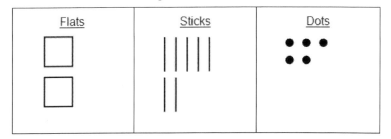

Flats	Sticks	Dots

Groups: 2 hundreds   7 tens   5 ones

Expanded Form: 200 + 70 + 5 = 275
(More Advanced, Alternative Answer is 2*100 + 7*10 + 5*1 = 275)

In addition to these rather simple examples, Expanded Form can also be used to describe much larger numbers without the use of Base Ten Blocks.

Example 5

Directions: Rewrite 347,842 in Expanded Form.

Answer to Example 5
300,000 + 40,000 + 7,000 + 800 + 40 + 2 = 347,842
(More Advanced, Alternate Answer is
3*100,000+4*10,000+7*1,000+8*100+4*10+2*1
=347,842)

Summary
In review, we have found that student success in mastering a conceptual understanding of large numbers and Place Value requires solid experience viewing and working with representations of number quantity, particularly for two- and three-digit numbers. However, even very young students can begin experimenting with number parts by Decomposing one- and two-digit numbers into smaller pairs using Tree Diagrams and Tape Diagrams. In its initial stages, these exercises form a basis for number comparison and basic addition. At its later stages, they become tools for discussing how to break any two digit number into groups of Tens and Ones.

Consider the following suggestions for how to better understand concepts related to Place Value:

1. The most common areas of confusion regarding this portion of grade K-2 math instruction are related to unfamiliar terminology, such as: Decomposing Numbers, Tree Diagram, Tape Diagram, and Expanded Form. Though the examples in this section are only representative of some ways in which these methods can be used to help students with place value, reviewing the definitions and examples in this chapter should help give a foundation for understanding their more basic uses.

2. Base Ten Blocks are often familiar to parents, but the newer, simplified names of "Flats, Sticks, and Dots" can be confusing when they are first introduced. Recall that Flats represent "100s", Sticks represent "10s", and Dots represent "1s". You can also search the internet for "Base Ten Block Printables" and use the abundance of resources available to make your own exercises at home. Make a game of creating and naming numbers together to help your child build an intuition about number size and the meaning of digits in large numbers.

3. When discussing large (especially two and three digit) numbers with your own child, check to see that they understand the direct connection between Base Ten Blocks and their ability to write numbers in expanded form. Students should build a solid foundation for their knowledge of larger numbers by practicing first with Base Ten Block representations. Once they are comfortable with this step, they should begin counting and naming the

groups of block as hundreds, tens, and ones. (Example: When modeling 438, they should be able to indicate that there are 4 hundreds, 3 tens, and 8 ones in this number.) Lastly, they should be able to state their number as an addition sentence, putting their number into Expanded Form. (Example: Represent 438 as 400+30+8.) It is important to explicitly show students that these three answers (438 as flats, sticks, and dots; 438 as hundreds, tens, and ones; and 438 as 400+30+8) are really the same activity written in three different ways. These models should *not* be introduced as three unrelated activities, since that would be more likely to confuse and overwhelm students rather than to help them. Describing these models as three ways of writing the same idea is much more concise, manageable, and meaningful.

For more specific details regarding the Common Core's structure for teaching place value, see the information provided by the Common Core State Standards Initiative (2015b) on their website under the section heading for "Numbers & Operations in Base Ten".

See the Math in action!
Check out the companion videos for *Chapter 4* at www.commoncoremath101.com.

Chapter 5

Addition and Subtraction

In many ways, Addition and Subtraction are two sides of the same coin, something that the Common Core Standards for Mathematics specifically emphasize in a variety of ways (Common Core State Standards Initiative, 2015c). To define more clearly what is meant by this, let us consider the addition statement: 4+5=9.

To help students become more fluent in using their knowledge of addition and subtraction interchangeably, it is important to present addition statements (and the unknown value) in multiple ways. Traditionally, addition practice problems place the "unknown value" as the *sum*, or the *result*, like this:

$$4 + 5 = ?$$

However, the Common Core State Standards also require teachers to present addition problems with unknown *addends*:

$$4 + ? = 9$$
$$? + 5 = 9$$

In the same way, Subtraction statements, like 9-5=4, should be presented in all three of the following ways:

$$9 - 5 = ?$$
$$9 - ? = 4$$
$$? - 5 = 4$$

One model that is especially helpful in building a strong foundation in addition and subtraction is the **Tape Diagram** (previously mentioned in *Chapter 4: Understanding Place Value*). Consider the following models as illustrations for the statements described above.

Example 1
True Addition Statement with Tape Diagram

Variety of Choices for Unknown Value

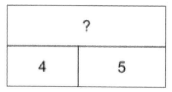

Could Represent: 4+5=? or ?-5=4

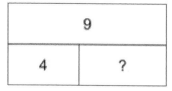

Could Represent: 4+?=9 or 9-?=4

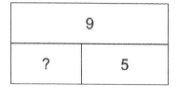

Could Represent: ?+5=9 or 9-5=?

Another important perspective that students should be taught about addition problems, is how to consider the multiple methods by which we can add to get a given sum when the addends have not been specified. In other words, students might be asked to consider the variety of ways that they might complete the statement: ? + ? = 9. In other words, can students create their own Tape Diagram given only the desired length?

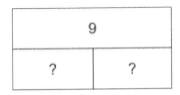

A math vocabulary term that is helping students to draw these connections between addition and subtraction with a variety of unknowns is the math phrase: **Adding On**. For instance, students should be able to interpret the expression of 4+5 as: *the quantity of four, adding on five more numbers -- which from 4 is 5, 6, 7, 8, 9 -- the total is 9.* Here we find that, instead of seeing basic Addition as just a jumbling of two random whole numbers, the term "Adding On" helps students to visualize addition in terms of a **Number Line** (or at younger ages, as a growing Tape Diagram), moving on from Zero to higher numbers. As an example, consider the following addition sentence, number line model, and verbal description.

<u>Example 2A</u>
Addition Sentence:
$$13 + 4 = ?$$

Number Line Model:

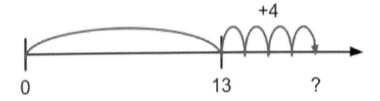

Verbal Description:
"The addition statement 13 + 4 asks us to find 13 on the
number line,
and then 'Add On' 4 more. (From 13, that is...14, 15, 16,
17.) Thus, 13 + 4 = 17."

Now suppose we use the same basic diagram, but change
the unknown to model the addition statement of 13 + ? = 17
(Example 2B) and again to model the addition statement of
? + 4 = 17 (Example 2C).

<u>Example 2B</u>
Addition Sentence:
13 + ? = 17

Number Line Model:

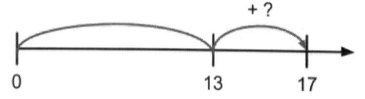

Verbal Description:
"How much must we Add On to 13 to get 17? (**Counting
On** from 13...14, 15, 16, 17.)
There are 4 jumps from 13 to 17, so the unknown value is
4."

Example 2C
Addition Sentence:
$? + 4 = 17$

Number Line Model:

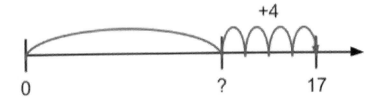

Verbal Description:
"If an unknown number plus 4 equals 17, we should be able to find the unknown by **Counting Back** 4 digits from 17 (...16, 15, 14, 13). The number that is 4 digits before 17 is 13. Therefore, the unknown value is 13."

Notice that, particularly in Example 2C, students will likely begin to use subtraction strategies to solve for the unknown without even being prompted by a teacher. These self initiated solution strategies are critical in helping students to develop intuitive, not just memorized, mathematical knowledge. It is also possible to utilize number lines to model subtraction problems explicitly. Consider the following examples.

Example 3A
Subtraction Sentence:
$17 - 4 = ?$

Number Line Model:

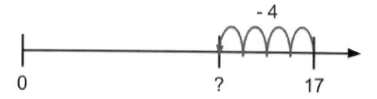

Verbal Description:
"The subtraction sentence 17 minus 4 asks us to take the number 17 and 'count back' 4 units to find the difference. Counting back from 17 we have...16, 15, 14, 13. Thus, 17 - 4 = 13."

<u>Example 3B</u>
Subtraction Sentence:
17 - ? = 13

Number Line Model:

Verbal Description:
"Here we are asked to 'count back' an unknown number of units from 17 until we reach 13. Counting back from 17 we have...16, 15, 14, 13. We counted back 4 units. Therefore, the unknown value is 4."

Subtraction Sentence:

? - 4 = 13

Number Line Model:

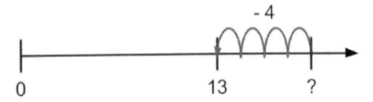

Verbal Description:

"If we 'count back' 4 units from an unknown number, the answer is 13. We could find the unknown value by 'adding on' 4 to 13, which is...14, 15, 16, 17.
Therefore, the original unknown value is 17."

Other Models and Manipulatives for Teaching Addition and Subtraction

Several of the Models and Manipulatives that were used to develop Number Sense (see *Chapter 3: Building Number Recognition and Intuition*) and Place Value Knowledge (see *Chapter 4: Understanding Place Value*) are also extremely valuable in bringing deeper understanding to the Addition and Subtraction Algorithms.

For smaller and more basic Addition Problems, **Ten Frames** are often used to give students something visual to scaffold their fact memorization. Consider the following example:

Example 4A
Double Ten Frame Template

Directions: Represent "8+6" on the Double Ten Frame, then solve.

Step1: Represent 8 and 6 Individually

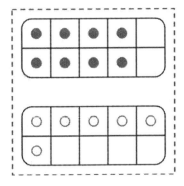

Step 2: Fill in Extra Spaces in Top Frame

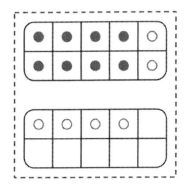

In the first diagram, a student is able to clearly identify the individual quantities of "8" and "6". To find the sum, they can move symbols from one Frame to the other until they clearly have "10" (a full frame) plus another number (in this case "4"). For parents who value speed in mathematical calculations, this exercise may seem unnecessarily complicated. Essentially, a student has just taken the basic addition sentence of "8+6", modeled it, turned it into the new addition sentence "10+4", and finally shown that the solution to both sentences is "14". It is important to recognize that the purpose of this exercise is *not* to solve the problem quickly. In fact, the exercise has nothing to do with developing an addition algorithm for future use. The purpose of this model is for students to be able to visualize the simple math so that they will eventually be able to complete the calculation with mental math. It highlights the importance of the benchmark "10" in completing simple addition problems. Suppose a student is later given a similar problem to solve, such as "7+5". Using mental math, they might consider that "7" is only 3 digits away from "10". If they mentally turn "7+5" into "7+3+2", they can quickly decide that the answer is One Group of 10, plus 2 extra (or simply "10+2"), which yields a total of "12". Once again, this model emphasizes the importance of **Making 10** when trying to solve basic math problems quickly (See also *Chapter 3: Building Number Recognition & Intuition*).

Next, let us consider how this same Double Ten Frame Template can be used to model simple subtraction.

Example 4B

Directions: Represent "14 - 6" on the Double Ten Frame,
then solve.

Step 1: Represent the quantity 14.

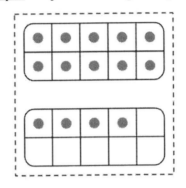

Step 2: Cross out 6 objects.

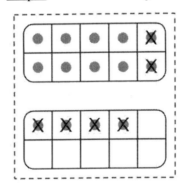

In the first diagram, we see that a student is able to model
the original quantity "14". In the second diagram, they
model the act of "subtracting", "taking away", or "crossing
out" the quantity "6". When students have completed the
model, they can clearly see that 14 - 6 = 8. Again, this
method is designed to help students internalize the process

of simple subtraction to strengthen their mental math skills. Using the method of **Making 10** in reverse, a student might see that "14" is only 4 units away from the value "10". Thus, they can rework the subtraction sentence in their head, knowing that "14 - 6" is the same as "14 - 4 - 2", or essentially "10 - 2". Teaching this kind of mental math would be quite complicated if taught symbolically, but with the Ten Frame Model, students are encouraged to create this kind of meaning more intuitively.

As students begin to add and subtract with two and three digit numbers, a more powerful model is needed to accommodate the larger numbers. **Base Ten Blocks** are the perfect tool for visualizing these higher level problems. Consider the following example:

Example 5A
Base Ten Blocks' Two Digit Addition Template

Sticks	Dots

Sticks	Dots

✛

*Directions: Model "23 + 54" with Base Ten Blocks,
then Solve.*

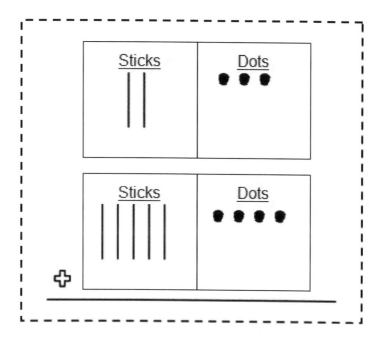

Using this diagram, students can clearly see that "sticks" (groups of 10) and "dots" (unit blocks) must be added separately according to their columns. We see that, in the "sticks" column, there are 2 tens and 5 tens that can be grouped to total 7 tens. In the "dots" column, we find 3 ones and 4 ones that can be grouped to total 7 ones. Thus, our sum is 7 tens and 7 ones, or $70 + 7 = 77$.

Next, let us consider what happens when the "dots" column yields a total of 10 or more.

Example 5B
Directions: Model "45+27" with Base Ten Blocks, then Solve.

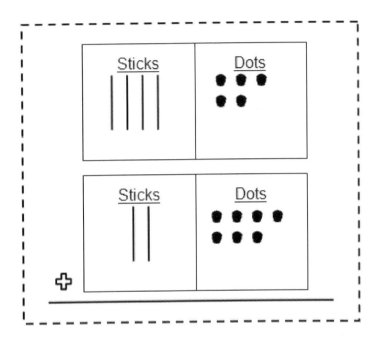

This time, if students combine their "sticks" and "dots" columns, they will run into a problem. There are a total of 6 tens and 12 ones. How can we write this as a number? When students learn the basics of Base Ten Blocks, they are taught the importance of looking for groups of 10 dots that can be "traded in" or "exchanged for 1 stick. If 10 dots equals 1 stick, then our answer to Example 5B can be modified from 6 sticks and 12 dots, to be 6 sticks and 1 stick with 2 dots. Note this process of **Making 10 (or Composing 10)** in the diagram below:

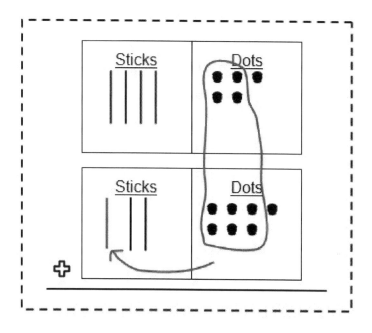

Notice that, once we convert the 10 dots to 1 stick, that quantity can be moved into the sticks' group or column. This should remind you of the older technique of "carrying a one" when adding larger numbers. We no longer use the phrase "carry the one", because it undermines the place value significance of "1" and can seem arbitrary to students. Truthfully, the carried "1" has a value of ten. Perhaps the phrase "carry the one" would have been more meaningful to us if we had called it "moving the ten" instead.

Returning to the result of Example 5B, we find that our solution of 6 tens and 1 ten with 2 dots becomes, more simply, 7 tens and 2 dots. This means that the solution is 70 and 2, giving a total of 72.

Let us consider one more example of this kind of problem before we move forward. This time, we will use three digit addends that require **Regrouping** in both the Ones and Tens columns.

<u>Example 5C</u>
Base Ten Blocks' Three Digit Addition Template

Flats	Sticks	Dots

Flats	Sticks	Dots

✚

Directions: Model "248+374" with Base Ten Blocks
then Solve.

Step 1: Model the Problem

Flats	Sticks	Dots
☐ ☐	‖‖‖‖	●●●● ●●●●

Flats	Sticks	Dots
☐ ☐ ☐	‖‖‖‖‖‖‖	●● ●●

Step 2: Make and Move Groups of 10

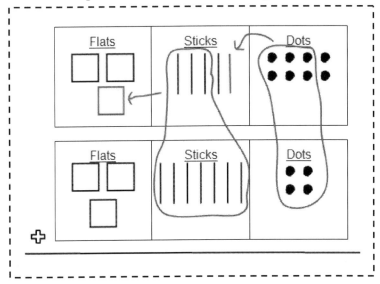

After **Regrouping** the 10 dots as 1 stick, and the 10 sticks as 1 flat, we now see that our sum includes: 6 flats, 2 sticks, and 2 dots. These represent the quantities 600, 20, and 2, showing that 248 + 374 = 622.

Base Ten Representations can also be used to model and solve subtraction problems. Regrouping is unnecessary when we subtract, in the same way that we never learned to "carry the 1" unless we were adding. Instead, subtraction of two- and three-digit numbers introduces the concept of "borrowing" (according to the old language of math teaching) or "decomposing" (according the new, place value conscious language). Consider the following examples:

Base Ten Blocks' Two Digit Subtraction Template

Sticks	Dots

Sticks	Dots

Directions: Model the Subtraction Sentence "64-32", and then Solve.

Step 1: Model the Sentence.

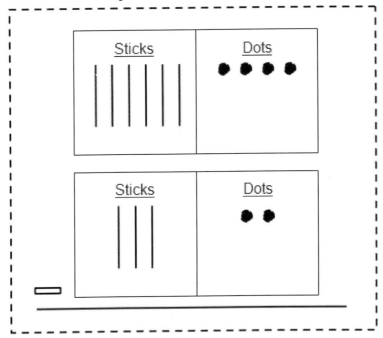

Step 2: Subtract the Bottom Quantity from the Top Quantity.

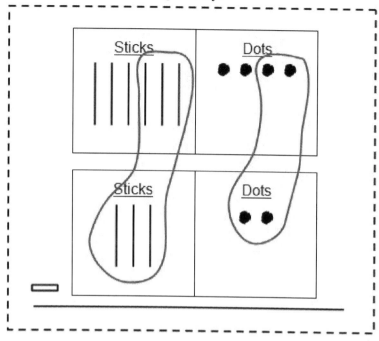

Step 3: Note what remains.

After Subtracting the lower quantity from the top quantity, we find that the amount remaining is simply: 3 tens and 2 ones. This is equivalent to 30 + 2 = 32.

Thus the solution to our subtraction problem is this:

64 - 32 = 32.

Notice that this problem does not require "borrowing". We simply take away the lower quantity from the top and find our solution. Now let us consider the subtraction sentence: "64 - 36 = ?".

<u>Example 6B</u>

Directions: Model the Subtraction Sentence "64 - 36" with Base Ten Blocks, then solve.

Step 1: Model the Sentence.

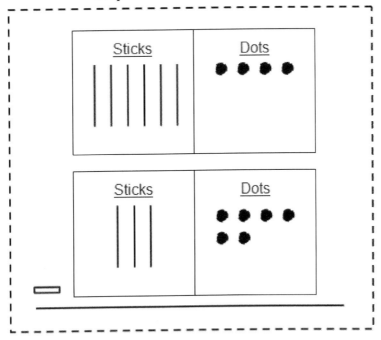

Now let us pause to consider the next step necessary for solving this problem. Step 2, as defined in Example 6A would require us to subtract, or cancel, the lower quantity from the top quantity. However, take notice that the number of "dots" in the lower model is *more than* the number of "dots" in the top model, so this is impossible. Here we must show students that we must "borrow" some dots from the sticks column. Except, we do not use the term borrow. Instead we tell them to **Decompose** one stick into dots. Knowing that one stick is equivalent to ten dots, they are able to complete this task and continue solving.

Step 2A: Decompose *One Stick* to Increase the number of Dots.

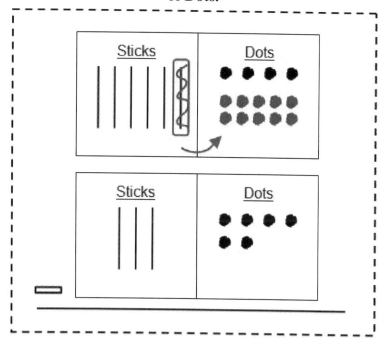

Step 2B: Subtract the Bottom Quantity from the Top Quantity.

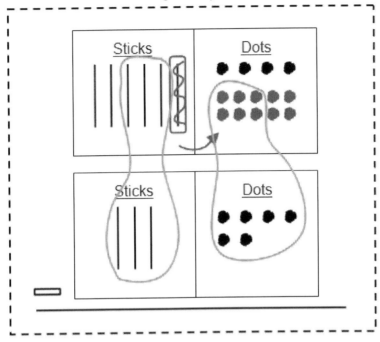

Step 3: Note what remains.

After Subtracting the lower quantity from the top quantity, we find that the amount remaining is simply: 2 tens and 8 ones. This is equivalent to 20 + 8 = 28.
Thus the solution to our subtraction problem is this:
64 - 36 = 28.

To solidify this material, let us consider one more example that requires "borrowing" or **Decomposing**. This time we will extend this knowledge to three digit numbers.

Example 6C

Base Ten Blocks' Two Digit Subtraction Template

Flats	Sticks	Dots

Flats	Sticks	Dots

Directions: Model the Subtraction Sentence "245-189",
and then Solve.

Step 1: Model the Sentence.

Step 2A: Decompose as Needed to allow for Subtraction.

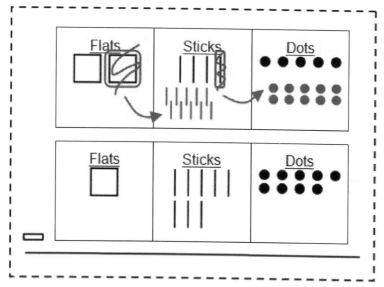

*Notice that this subtraction problem requires Extra Dots and Extra Sticks. Thus, we **Decompose** one stick into ten dots, and we Decompose one flat into ten sticks.*

Step 2B: Subtract the Bottom Quantity from the Top Quantity.

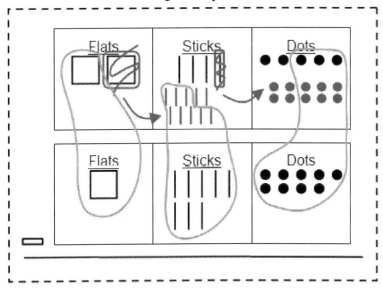

Step 3: Note what remains.

After Subtracting the lower quantity from the top quantity, we find that the amount
remaining is: 0 hundreds, 8 tens, and 6 ones. This is equivalent to 80 + 6 = 86.
Thus the solution to our subtraction problem is this: 245 - 189 = 56.

As is typical with any math model used to learn new operations, there is a point where the complexity of the model becomes more trouble than it is worth. One glance at Example 6C above shows just how cluttered a student's worksheet will eventually become using the Base Ten Blocks, unless a more concise algorithm is taught. This next step towards a more traditional method of solving larger addition and subtraction problems is a method called **Partial Sums**. It incorporates the ideas of Base Ten Blocks with students' knowledge about writing numbers in **Expanded Form** (see also *Chapter 4: Understanding Place Value*). Recall that multi-digit numbers can be written according to their place value as follows: 245 = 200 + 40 + 5 and 189 = 100 + 80 +9. Now consider how we might add these two numbers using the expanded form.

<u>Example 7A</u>
Directions: Solve the Addition Sentence "245 + 189" using Partial Sums.

```
    245                    200 + 40 + 5
  + 189          ⟶      +  100 + 80 + 9
  ───────                ──────────────────
                          300 + 120 + 14 = 434
```

By writing our addition sentence in the Partial Sum Form, students have a couple key advantages. Firstly, they do not have to worry about "carrying" extra numbers. For instance, using the traditional algorithm, we would first add the ones column to get 5+9=14. We would write the four below the ones column and then "carry the 1" to the second column -- if that sounds a bit confusing, you might be on to something. Many young students struggle to remember this step of "carrying the 1", because they do not have a conceptual basis for why this step needs to be done. The Partial Sums method allows students to add these numbers in the same way that they would add/combine Base Ten Blocks. They combine according to Place Value "groups" and then find the total of all the parts.

I have also seen some teachers ask students to complete Partial Sums without splitting the number into its place value pieces. Though I personally find this alternative method a bit confusing and less intuitive for younger students, I want to include an example for the parents who may see this type of question in their students' work.

Example 7B Alternative Method
Directions: Solve the Addition Sentence "245 + 189" using Partial Sums.

$$
\begin{array}{r}
245 \\
+\quad 189 \\
\hline
\end{array}
$$

300	*hundreds column total*
120	*tens column total*
+ 14	*ones column total*

$$
434
$$

These same ideas can also be used to solve subtraction problems symbolically using **Partial Differences**. Consider how we might use Expanded Form to solve the Subtraction Sentence "245 - 189=?" in the following example:

<u>Example 8A</u>
Directions: Solve the Subtraction Sentence "245 - 189"
using Partial Sums.

$$
\begin{array}{r}
245 \\
- \quad 189 \\
\hline
\end{array}
\longrightarrow
\begin{array}{r}
200 + 40 + 5 \\
- \quad 100 + 80 + 9 \\
\hline
100 - 40 - 4 = 60 - 4 = 56
\end{array}
$$

Note that, in Example 8A, moving from left to right, we find that "200 - 100 = 100", "40 - 80 = -40", and "5 - 9 = -4". These "Partial" answers can be combined to find the actual solution of "56". Note that, we could see the appearance of numbers like "-40" and "-4" as an introduction to the idea of negative integers (something a bit too advanced for younger students), or we can look at this method as a way to reinforce the idea that, after subtracting, we still have 40 extra objects that need to be taken away from the top number. If we had modeled this subtraction sentence with Base Ten Blocks (See Example 6C), students would have found that there were 4 "sticks" (tens) left over in the bottom row and nothing left in the top row to subtract them from. At that point, students would "borrow" or "decompose" a flat block into 10 sticks to complete the computation. With Partial Differences, students can do this same work more simply by computing their final subtraction sentence of "100 - 40 - 4" to get "56".

Consider this same Subtraction Sentence completed in the alternative method for **Partial Differences**.

<u>Example 8B</u>

Directions: Solve the Subtraction Sentence "245 - 189"
using Partial Differences.

```
    245
 -  189
```

```
    100   left over after subtracting hundreds column
  - 40    left over after subtracting tens column
   - 4    left over after subtracting ones column
```

```
    56
```

This procedure utilizes the same logic described in Example 8A but organizes the information vertically instead of horizontally.

Summary

The handful of newer ideas and methods for teaching addition and subtraction strongly reflects a well-respected teaching method referred to as "C-R-A" or "Concrete-Representational-Abstract" (Sousa, 2008, p. 186; Van de Walle, Karp, & Bay-Williams, 2013, pp. 99-100). This method seeks to bring deep and lasting meaning to educational concepts by presenting material in three important ways: as *concrete* realities that can be modeled with actual objects; as something visual that can be *represented* with a picture, graph or other drawing; and as an *abstract* concept that can be described with symbols, numbers, mathematical signs, or letters. The C-R-A method is an ordered process, not just a handful of different ways to teach. Good practice of this method should follow roughly the following steps over an extended period of time (in other words, think of this process in terms of days not minutes or hours):

Step 1: Concrete
New concepts are first introduced using concrete models and objects that allow for structured experimentation of the topic. The purpose is to create meaningful connections between the real world and mathematical ideas.

Step 2: Concrete and Representational
Students use models to solve a mathematical problem and then draw pictures, graphs, or some other written representation as a record of their work with the concrete objects.

Step 3: Representational
Students show that they can solve the mathematical problems using pencil, paper, and drawings without the help of the concrete objects.

Step 4: Representational and Abstract
Students continue to use drawings to find solutions and make meaning of math problems, but teachers begin introducing and requiring the use of traditional math symbols in each of their answers.

Step 5: Abstract
Students show that they can solve mathematical problems using only symbolic methods.

Note that the ultimate goal of the C-R-A method is to help students master the symbolic (or, in other words, the more traditional) way of solving math problems. However, the deliberate, multi-step process of building that knowledge in stages, from Concrete to Representational to Abstract, is especially important in helping struggling students to master and remember what they have learned (Sousa, 2008). One of the most common parental concerns regarding the type of material discussed in this chapter is that the increased focus on using models and drawings to teach key algorithms, such as addition and subtraction, will render their child unfit to do math in the real world, where people almost always use traditional, symbolic methods. However, these unconventional methods actually help students to form a strong and memorable foundation of mathematical understanding, based on real-world meaning, that will eventually make it easier to learn, recall, and correctly perform the traditional methods and algorithms.

In reflecting on the research regarding both C-R-A and the math methods discussed in this chapter, consider these suggestions for how to advocate for quality instruction of addition and subtraction in grades K-2:

1. Teaching of Addition and Subtraction techniques should follow a deliberate Concrete-Representational-Abstract progression. This does not mean that a student who can perform abstract, symbolic addition should *never* practice again with concrete methods. However, it does mean that teachers should be intentional about the order with

which they present the connections and progression from one method to the next. Simply teaching a bunch of "new methods" with no explanation of their connections to one another will likely create more confusion than help. Here is a sample progression that a teacher might use to teach addition with sums less than or equal to 20:

- Introduce basic addition using Double Ten Frames and color chips that can be physically moved to find the sum. (Concrete)
- Have students add with the physical Ten Frames and color chips and then record a picture of their work and solution with colored pencils and paper. (Concrete-Representational)
- Students begin to solve addition problems with colored pencils and paper Ten Frame grids but no physical model (such as the color chips). (Representational)
- Students use paper and pencil with Ten Frame grids to solve, then they write the symbolic expression next to their work. (Representational-Abstract)

Representational-Abstract Example:

Representational

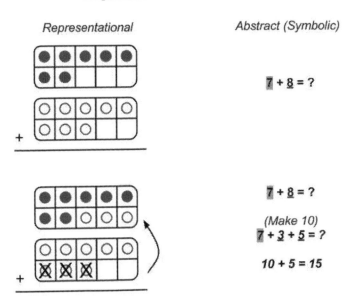

Abstract (Symbolic)

7 + 8 = ?

7 + 8 = ?

(Make 10)
7 + 3 + 5 = ?

10 + 5 = 15

- Lastly, students demonstrate that they can perform simple addition (sums less than or equal to 20) using number symbols only. (Abstract)

Notice that this progression addresses one specific type of addition problem and deliberately moves from the use of concrete tools towards abstract (symbolic) solution techniques. Students would be able to fall back on prior methods if they became stuck at any point, but the teacher leads the student towards symbolic methods as the end goal. Keep in mind that this process takes days (at least) to do well. If students are pushed too quickly from one step to the next, the C-R-A method loses its effectiveness. Similarly, if teachers fail to use the C-R-A method (or a similar progression) at all, the alternative algorithms themselves lose their meaning and effectiveness. Our goal is *not* to make addition seem more complicated by giving students a dozen different methods for solving. The goal is to lead them from concrete, meaningful experiences towards abstract, symbolic solution methods that will be useful for the rest of their time as students of mathematics.

2. In further consideration of the C-R-A method as it applies to addition and subtraction, I would also strongly advocate that the Partial Sums and Partial Differences Methods should *only* be taught after and in conjunction with the concrete Base Ten Block Methods. Ideally, the C-R-A progression should be something like this *(note: two-digit and three-digit number examples as well as addition and subtraction operations should each be taught in separate C-R-A progressions even though they are described together in the following outline)*:

    -   Students experiment with physical Base Ten Blocks as a method for solving two and three digit addition or subtraction problems. (Concrete)
    -   Students solve with Base Ten Blocks and then use paper and pencil to record a picture of their work as dots, sticks, and flats. (Concrete-Representational)
    -   Students demonstrate that they can use paper and pencil to draw diagrams of dots, sticks,

and flats without needing to use the physical Base Ten Blocks. (Representational)

- Students use paper and pencil to show diagrams of dots, sticks, and flats, and then write their solution out symbolically using Partial Sums or Partial Differences. (Representational-Abstract)

- Students demonstrate that they can solve using just the symbolic method of Partial Sums or Partial Differences. (Abstract)

Once students are working fluently with Partial Sums or Partial Differences, it is an appropriate time to introduce the traditional algorithms for addition and subtraction. They have enough background knowledge at this point to make sense of its structure. However, it is still advised that we use language like "regrouping" or "decomposing" instead of "carry the one" or "borrowing", since those phrases do not clearly reference the work they have done with physical models like Base Ten Blocks.

3. If you want to help your student begin practicing addition and subtraction problems in meaningful ways, you can make double Ten Frames from two old egg cartons with one row of two removed (so that each carton is 2x5). Using two different colored dried beans (or any other objects of two different colors), students can work on examples like the ones shown in this chapter at home. Also, if you want to work with two and three digit addition and subtraction models, there are an abundance of free

Base Ten Block printable resources available on the internet if you make a simple search of the phrase "Base Ten Block Printables". This is a helpful way for parents to help their children to practice from home using a familiar method.

For more specific details regarding the Common Core's Standards for teaching addition and subtraction, see the information provided by the Common Core State Standards Initiative (2015b) on their website under the section headings for "Operations & Algebraic Thinking" and "Number & Operations in Base Ten".

See the Math in action!
Check out the companion videos for *Chapter 5* at www.commoncoremath101.com.

Chapter 6
Statistics Foundation (Organizing Data)

Professionals in the field of Math Education in the United States continue to develop and review our effectiveness at preparing students for future careers, attention has been increasingly drawn to the current importance of Statistics Knowledge for students going into *any* career after completing school. Because of this, the Common Core Standards have incorporated discussion about Data Organization as early as Kindergarten (Common Core State Standards Initiative, 2015b, see Kindergarten: Measurement & Data section). In Grades K-2, there are three types of data organizing charts/diagrams/graphs that students are expected to be able to utilize and interpret appropriately.

Picture Graph

The simplest and most intuitive data organizer considered in this chapter is the **Picture Graph**. Consider the following example of this type of chart:

Example 1

Directions: Organize the following data into the picture graph below.

Though the Picture Graph is a rather uncomplicated, simplistic method for discussing data, it is an invaluable tool for helping young students learn how to organize and make visual judgements about a group of objects. It creates something concrete that can be used to stimulate classroom (or homework related) discussions about the concepts of: Most, Least, More Than, Less Than, etc.

Line Plot

Contrary to the Picture Graph, a **Line Plot** is a more numbers-oriented technique for data organization. Consider the following example:

Example 2
Directions: Construct a Line Plot for the following set of data.
(5, 4, 1, 2, 3, 9, 6, 4, 3, 2, 3, 5, 5)

Step 1: If the question does not already include a pre-drawn, empty Line Plot, students must construct one that includes an appropriate range of numbers. Given the data set described in this example, it would be appropriate to construct a Plot of numbers 0 through 10.

Step 2: Plot each data value above its corresponding number.

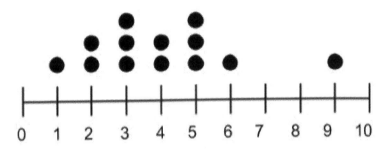

As Example 2 clearly shows, a **Line Plot** is another very basic and simplistic tool for data organization. It is useful for modeling small sets of data that include whole numbers only. However, it allows young students to visually connect to statistical ideas like: Most Common Value (Mode), Middle Value (Median), or Unusual Value (Outlier). In this particular example (Example 2), we find that the *Most Common Values* are "3" and "5" since they have the same number of dots. The *Middle Value* is "4", since there are 13 dots total and the middle one (the 7th dot) is located above the number "4". And lastly, we find that the most *Unusual*

Value is "9", since it is clearly "out of place" relative to the rest of the data.

Bar Graph

Most parents probably recall creating and analyzing bar graphs during their own elementary school days. However, as a brief refresher, let us consider Example 3A and 3B to see how this Data Organizer compares to the Picture Graph and Line Plot.

Example 3A
Directions: Create a Bar Graph to model the data set from Example 1.

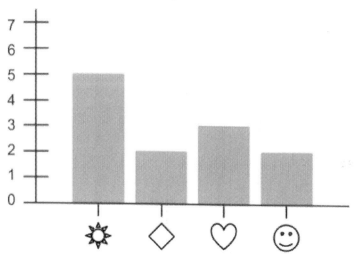

Example 3B

Directions: Create a Bar Graph to model the data set from Example 2.

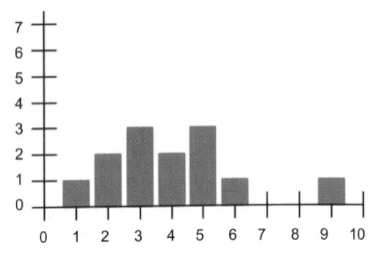

The **Bar Graph** is really the first data organizer that has long term potential for students. It is flexible in its ability to describe groups of objects or groups of numbers. It can eventually be used to represent quantities that have decimal or fractional values, not just whole numbers. It is also easily scalable to represent large amounts, say hundreds or thousands of objects, something that neither Picture Graphs nor Line Plots are able to do. Lastly, we notice that Bar Graphs introduce students to the idea of two axes (vertical information and horizontal information in the same graph), something that will have long term application to their Middle School years.

Summary

While the material mentioned in this section is generally familiar and unlikely to cause much controversy, it is significant because it reflects an important shift and point of emphasis brought by the Common Core State Standards. When students ask math teachers, "When will we use all this math in real life anyway?", the answer is not always as obvious as when we discuss statistics. Our culture and the workplaces in our nation are saturated with statistics-related information. From television advertisements to scientific research, the need for a solid understanding of statistics and the ability to appropriately discuss and assess data is evident *everywhere*. There are two important take-aways from this chapter:

1. Statistics is no longer a word for just high school and college students. This topic is too important to "save for later", and even Kindergarteners are going to be asked to make their attempts at organizing and interpreting data in an age appropriate fashion.

2. When it comes to data interpretation, the "real world" has already made it abundantly clear that the way that you present data can greatly influence the way other people understand and accept it. Two politicians can use the same data to make countering points. How is that possible? Usually it means that one or both groups are choosing to focus on different aspects of the data available to them, thus coming to opposite conclusions. It is absolutely critical that we teach our students to be able to do more than just organize data; they need to be able to

take the information and discuss, analyze, agree, and disagree with each other over it. Teacher and parent initiated discussions of how to organize and interpret data, even with young children, is essential in helping train students how to put their statistics knowledge to good use in the real world.

For more specific details regarding the Common Core's emphasis on data presentation in the early grades, see the information provided by the Common Core State Standards Initiative (2015b) on their website under the section heading for "Measurement & Data".

See the Math in action!
Check out the companion videos for *Chapter 6* at www.commoncoremath101.com.

Section 2

Challenging and New Material
Grades 3-5

Chapter 7
Multiplication and Division

In my own personal experience of processing parental feedback to "New Math" and "Changes Perpetuated by Common Core", the topics of Multiplication and Division are among the most commonly referenced areas of confusion and frustration. In the decade of my studies and experience with Math Education, I have already seen a number of changes made to the way that teachers are being instructed to teach basic Multiplication and Division. This is most likely because students have notoriously struggled to correctly memorize and apply the traditional algorithms that have been taught for ages. Even before the adoption of Common Core by many states, educators were beginning to adjust their methods of explaining and practicing these two basic operations. The Common Core State Standards simply made these more effective methods of teaching and describing Multiplication and Division a requirement for all states following their guidelines. It is important to remember that these "New Ideas" really are not entirely new. They are not meant to completely replace the value or practice of traditional Multiplication and Division Algorithms. Instead, like other Standards from the Common Core, the new methods are meant to develop a deeper, more lasting understanding of the concepts, allowing students to locate their own errors more quickly and to develop related math ideas more easily.

The main problem with these "new methods" is that parents often feel left in the dark when they review their child's homework. No adult appreciates the experience of looking at a 3rd or 4th grade math assignment and feeling stupid. If that has been your experience, let me begin by assuring you that – you are not stupid (hopefully you already knew that) – and neither is the math. We just need to take some time to bring clarity to the "whys" and "hows" of these newer practices.

Defining Multiplication in an Accurate and Useful Way
What is Multiplication? In decades past, we might have been more or less content to refer to it simply as the memorization of "Times Tables" on flash cards. The obvious problem with this definition is that – it really does nothing to explain *what* it is or *why* it works. Students with a stronger intuition for math might be able to figure out the

"Why" part on their own, but this is a poor teaching method since it alienates the aforementioned 50% of students (see Chapter 1: "Look for and make use of structure.") who do not have the same confidence or understanding. A better way to teach this concept is to model Multiplication in the following way:

3×4 means 3 groups of 4 objects
(or...)

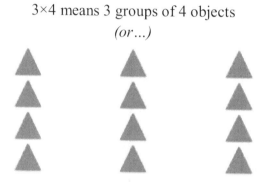

If we can draw a picture to model a multiplication sentence, then we should also be able to *create* our own multiplication sentence if we are given a visual **Array** of objects (see also *Chapter 3: Building Number Recognition and Intuition*). Consider the following Array:

Example 1

There are many ways to explore the number of objects pictured in Example 1. When students are first learning about multiplication, they might be inclined to view the Array from the perspective of addition. If asked to find the total number of objects they might do any of the following:

1) Count the objects one by one to find a total of 15.
2) Visualize the Array as two groups, perhaps as 6 and 9.

This means we have 6+9=15 objects.

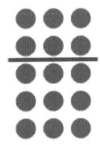

3) Visualize the Array as three or more groups, perhaps as 6, 6, and 3.

This means we have 6+6+3=15 objects.

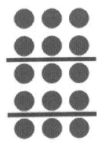

When we break a group of objects into smaller pieces, it becomes easier to calculate the total number of objects. What happens if we try to break this group into a handful of

Equal smaller groups? There are two ways that this can be accomplished.

Method 1

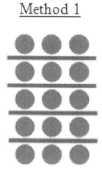

Horizontal Partitions
5 Groups of 3

Method 2

Vertical Partitions
3 Groups of 5

Using Method 1, we find that this Array can be described as "5 Equal Groups of 3", or 3+3+3+3+3=15. Multiplication gives us a shorthand way of writing the same things with new symbolism: 5 groups of 3 is the same as 5×3. Since we know that this Array has 15 objects from our prior calculations, we also know that 5×3=15. Similarly, by Method 2, we find that this Array can be described as "3 Equal Groups of 5", of 5+5+5=15. Using our new symbolism for Multiplication, we find that 3 groups of 5 is the same as 3×5, and thus 3×5=15 as well. Here we have established a useful definition of Multiplication while simultaneously proving the Commutative Property of Multiplication – a fancy way of saying that 5×3=3×5, or more generally, $a×b=b×a$. Instead of using flashcard quizzes and abstract definitions as the foundation of teaching multiplication, we have allowed the student to see "Why" it all works for themselves.

Multiplication and Area Models

After students become confident in utilizing the Array Model to describe multiplication, it is important to help them understand the connection between multiplication and area. Consider the following example:

Example 2A

Directions: Find the area of the rectangle.

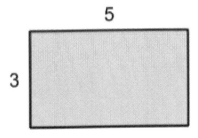

The most basic way of calculating Area is to partition a two dimensional shape into a grid of unit sized (1×1) squares and find the total number of squares that fit within the figure.

Example 2A cont.
...with unit squares drawn.

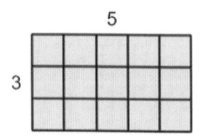

Using this definition and extra structure for finding area, we can now calculate the total number of unit squares in a variety of ways. In fact, we can use any of the same methods employed to find the total number of objects in the Array of Example 1. We can add one by one or by groups, but whatever method we choose, we will always find a total of 15, so we know that the area of this figure is 15 square units. Using our beginning knowledge of Multiplication, we also know that we could view this area in equal groups, either as 3 rows of 5 units (3×5=15) or as 5 columns of 3 units (5×3=15). This basic calculation and illustration is what we would call a simple **Area Model** of multiplication.

Now that we have clarified the relationship between multiplication and area, we can consider more complex examples. For instance:

Example 2B
Directions: Use multiplication to find the area of the rectangle.

16

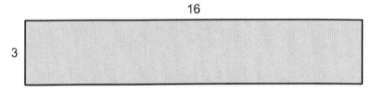

3

The simplest multiplication sentences that could be used to describe the area of this rectangle are: 3×16 (3 rows of 16 units) or 16×3 (16 columns of 3 units). However, neither of these multiplication sentences are likely to be familiar to a young student and might require a rather lengthy process to solve. However, we can simplify our calculation by splitting this large rectangle into two more manageable pieces.

Example 2B cont.
...partitioned to simplify calculations.

10   6

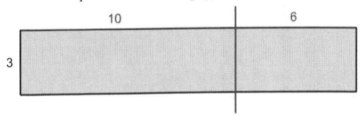

3

Note that, although we have altered the way that the rectangle is labeled, we have not changed the actual size or area of the figure. Thus, it would be mathematically valid to calculate the two small rectangles separately and add to find the original rectangle's total.

...find the area of the regions using simple multiplication facts.

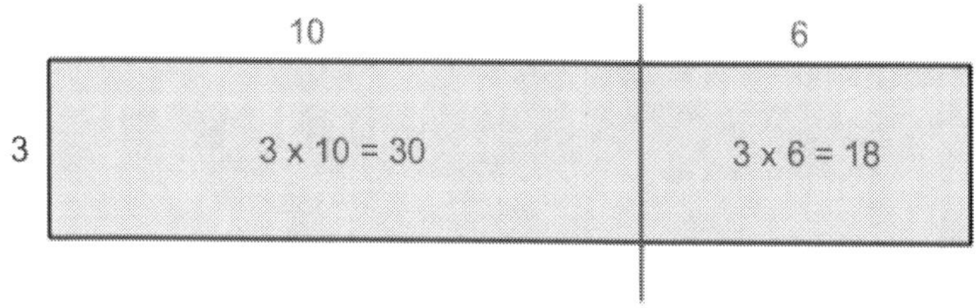

10	6
3 x 10 = 30	3 x 6 = 18

with "3" labeling the left side height.

Thus we find that the total area of our original figure must be 30 square units plus 18 square units. Since 30+18=48, the area must be 48 square units. This exercise shows that "3x16" is the same as "3×10 + 3×6", and that both multiplication sentences equal 48. However, the second sentence is much easier to complete using mental math (math done quickly in our head), because we are able to use familiar multiplication facts to find the total. Let us consider one more example of this kind of "simplification" technique for multiplication.

Example 2C
Directions: Use multiplication to find the area of the rectangle.

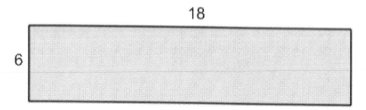

Step 1: Partition into smaller rectangles with simpler dimensions.

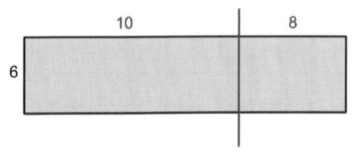

Step 2: Find the area of the smaller rectangles.

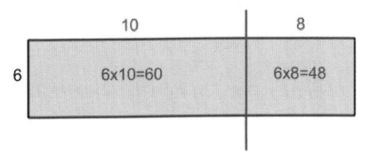

Step 3: Add the area of the parts to find the area of the whole.

If the left rectangle has an area of 60 square units, and the right rectangle has an area of 48 square units, then the total area is 60+48 or 108 square units.

Thus, we have also demonstrated that "6×18" is equivalent to "6×10 + 6×8", and both multiplication sentences equal 108.

Essentially, we have shown that, when finding the area of a rectangle with a one-digit dimension and a two digit dimension, we can partition the rectangle into two pieces to simplify the calculations necessary to find the total area. This same method of partitioning can also help us find the area of rectangles with two double-digit dimensions.

Example 2D

Directions: Use multiplication to find the area of the rectangle.

17

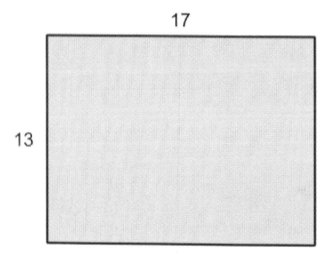

13

Step 1: Partition the rectangle to simplify calculations.
(This time we will use both *Vertical* and *Horizontal*
partitions.)

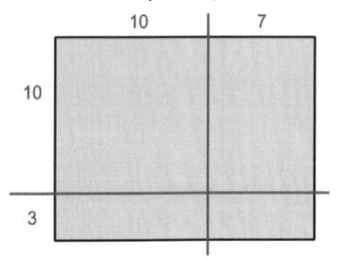

Note that, because our vertical and horizontal dimensions
are both two-digit values, we have made a vertical and a
horizontal partition to simplify the calculations. This
creates four smaller rectangles, each having an area that
should be easy to calculate with mental math.

<u>Example 2D cont.</u>
Step 2: Find the area of the four rectangle pieces.

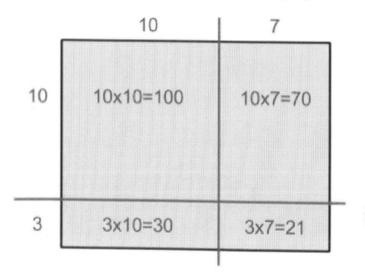

Step 3: Add the smaller areas to find the area of the original figure.
Since the areas of the smaller rectangles are 100 square units, 70 square units, 30 square units, and 21 square units, the large original rectangle must have an area of 100+70+30+21 square units. Thus, the area of the rectangle is 221 square units.

While this exercise is helpful in understanding how to simplify area problems, the goal of practicing this method with students is to create a basis of understanding for a Multiplication procedure that is often referred to as the **Box Method** (or simply the **Area Model** for multiplication). The method is exactly the same as shown in Examples 2A, 2B, 2C, and 2D. The only difference is that we don't need to worry about labeling "units" for area, because the purpose is finding a product not an area. To further establish the value of this method, let us first consider the traditional algorithm used for finding products of two digit numbers.

<u>Example 3A</u>

Directions: Find the product of 49×57 using the traditional algorithm.

$$
\begin{array}{r}
{}^{4}\!\!\!\!\!\!\!{}^{6} \\
49 \\
\times\ 57 \\
\hline
343 \\
+\ 2450 \\
\hline
2793
\end{array}
$$

Recall that the traditional multiplication algorithm includes ideas like "carrying" numbers (such as the small 6 and 4 in the upper left corner), adding a random "0" to the second addend to make sure numbers are aligned correctly, and multiplying one-digit numbers like "7x9", ""7x4", "5x9", and "5x4". None of these steps are explained conceptually, and students are generally expected to simply commit the steps to memory.

There is nothing wrong with the traditional algorithm for multiplication. In fact, it can be very useful for making quick on-paper calculations, as long as it is performed correctly. Thus, before teaching this rather abstract, memorization-based algorithm, students should experiment with the possibilities of a method called **Partial Products** (see Example 3B) and then make comparisons to the traditional algorithm for the sake of conceptual understanding.

Consider the following example of **Partial Products** and compare the process to the traditional Example shown in 3A.

Example 3B

Directions: Find the solution to the multiplication sentence 49×57 using Partial Products.

Step 1: Construct an empty Partial Products Box and choose which side will represent each of the factors from the multiplication sentence.

(57)

(49)

Step 2: Break each factor into smaller pieces that will be easy to multiply.

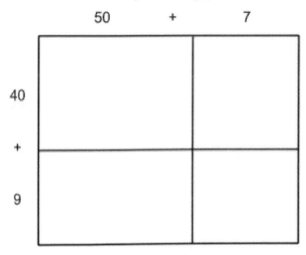

*Step 3: Find the **Partial Products** (in other words, the "area" of each small rectangle).*

	50 +	7
40	40x50=2000	40x7=280
+ 9	9x50=450	9x7=63

Step 4: The solution to the original multiplication sentence is the sum of
*the **Partial Products** (in other words, the "area" of the figure).*

The Partial Products are 2000, 280, 450, and 63. Since these sum to 2793, the solution to our original question is this: 49×57=2793.

Take a moment to compare Example 3A and Example 3B:

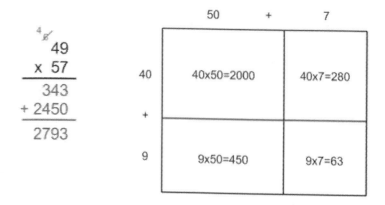

Notice that, for the traditional approach, the value "343" is actually the total of the right hand column in the Partial Products Box (280+63). Similarly, the value "2450" is the total found in the left hand column of the Partial Products Box (2000+450). As a bridge between the Box Method for Partial Products and the Traditional Algorithm, teachers may use symbolic models like Example 4C (below) to help students transition:

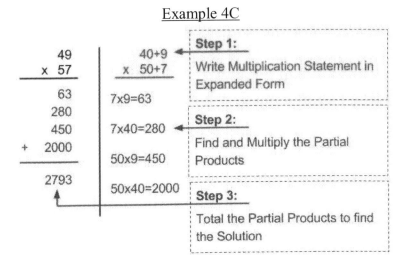

Example 4C

		Step 1:
49	40+9	Write Multiplication Statement in Expanded Form
x 57	x 50+7	
63	7x9=63	
280		Step 2:
450	7x40=280	Find and Multiply the Partial Products
+ 2000	50x9=450	
2793	50x40=2000	
		Step 3: Total the Partial Products to find the Solution

Here we see that the **Box Method for Partial Products**, the **Symbolic Method for Partial Products**, and the **Traditional Multiplication Algorithm** all yield the same answer using very similar calculations. The biggest difference between Partial Products and the Traditional Algorithm is that, Partial Products (whether the Box or the Symbolic Method) allows students to see exactly where each value comes from, and provides a clear answer to "Why" multiplication works. Ultimately, students will learn the traditional method because of its usefulness in quickly calculating very large products. However, as has already been established, we know that students perform better when they understand *why* math works. The Partial Products method is an attempt to make students' future work with traditional methods more accurate and easier to understand.

Defining Division and its Relationship to Multiplication

The new developments in Division are similar, and in many ways complementary to our previous discussion about Multiplication. First, we must agree that Division is the process of partitioning a set of objects into a given number of equal groups and finding the amount in each group, or alternatively, it is the process of partitioning a set of objects into groups of a certain number and then finding the total number of groups. At the same time, the Division operation is also directly related to Multiplication in that, given a Division statement such as "24÷6=?", it can be rewritten as a Multiplication statement such as "6×?=24" where one factor is unknown. This relationship between Multiplication and Division allows students to use knowledge of arrays, area, and partial products to accentuate and develop their understanding of division.

In my experience as a math student, tutor, and teacher, I have found that the topic of "Long Division" is rarely a favorite among students. This is probably partly due to the rather tedious nature of long division, but also because it was typically taught using the traditional "memorize and regurgitate" format that leaves students uncertain of why their work is meaningful or sensible. This is the reason that the method for teaching Division is changing. As always, the goal is to establish a foundation of understanding before asking students to simply memorize a traditional algorithm. First let us consider a few concrete ways of modeling Division according to its definition.

<u>Example 1A</u>

Directions: Model 18÷3 as 18 objects partitioned into 3 equal groups. Then solve.

<u>Group 1</u> <u>Group 2</u> <u>Group 3</u>

1	2	3
4	5	6
7	8	9
10	11	12
13	14	15
16	17	18

The solution to "18÷3" is "6", because there are 6 objects in each group.

<u>Example 1B</u>
Directions: Model 18÷3 as 18 objects partitioned into groups of 3. Then solve.

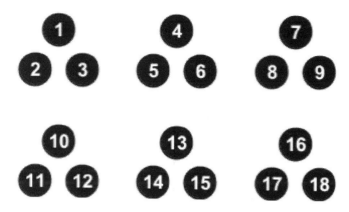

The solution to "18÷3" is "6",
because there are 6 groups of 3.

<u>Example 1C</u>
Directions: Rewrite 18÷3=? as a Multiplication Sentence, and solve for the unknown value.

<u>Solution:</u> 18÷3=? is the same as 3×?=18
The unknown value must be "6" since 3×6=18.

Long Division and Partial Quotients

Now that we have established the definition of Division, we must also consider the need for more efficient methods of solving division problems that involve large numbers. While "18" is an easy number to break into groups of 3 using a picture or model, the same cannot be said for a number like 378. Let us consider how many groups of 9 there are in 378, or in symbolic terms, let us calculate $378 \div 9$ using both traditional and newer methods.

Example 2A: Traditional Long Division

```
      42
   _____
 9 | 378
   -36↓
   _____
     18
    -18
   _____
      0
```

In Traditional Long Division, we compare the outside number (9) to each digit of the inside number (378). We ask, "How many 9s are in 3?" and if this is an impossible question, we move to the next digit and ask, "How many 9s are in 37?" We write our answer to these questions at the top. Then we find the remaining value and bring down the next digit and continue to ask the same question until we run out of digits.

The number at the top (42) is our solution.

Now that we have reviewed the traditional Long Division Method, let us compare it to the newer **Partial Quotient Method** which aims to support a student's journey to understand division as it relates to multiplication and the partitioning of numbers into equal groups.

Example 2B: Partial Quotient Method

```
9 | 378
  -180 | 20
  ----
   198
```

STEP 1:
Student asks,
"How many groups of 9 might fit into 378?"

Guess: "Maybe 20?"

Check: 20 groups of 9; 9x20=180

Student reflects,
"Close, but not enough. Let's see how much I still have to make into groups of 9."

Subtract: 378-180=198
Remaining quantity to be grouped is 198.

```
9 | 378
  -180 | 20
  ----
   198
  -180 | 20
  ----
    18
```

STEP 2:
Student asks,
"How many groups of 9 might fit into 198?"

Guess: "At least 20 more."

Check: 20 groups of 9; 9x20=180

Student reflects,
"Close, but still not enough. Let's see how much I still have to make into groups of 9."

Subtract: 198-180=18
Remaining quantity to be grouped is 18.

```
       42
   ┌───────
 9 │ 378
   │ -180  │ 20
   │ ───────
   │  198
   │ -180  │ 20
   │ ───────
   │   18
   │  -18  │ 2
   │ ───────
   │    0
```

STEP 3:
Student asks,
"How many groups of 9 might fit into 18?"

Guess: "I know that! Exactly 2."

Check: 2 groups of 9; 2x9=18

Student reflects,
"Perfect! I have grouped 378 into 20+20+2 groups of 9. This means there are 42 groups of 9 in 378."

Solution: 378 divided by 9 equals 42

When documented step by step, the Partial Quotient Method can look a bit daunting. For clarity's sake, consider Example 2C below, which reflects a possible solution to the division sentence "252÷6" and shows *only* the work that a student would record on their paper.

Example 2C

```
         43
     ┌───────
   6 │ 258
     │ - 60  │ 10        6x10=60
     │ ───────
     │  198
     │ -120  │ 20        6x20=120
     │ ───────
     │   78
     │  -60  │ 10        6x10=60
     │ ───────
     │   18
     │  -18  │ 3         6x3=18
     │ ───────
     │    0
```

In summary, the **Partial Quotients** method for Division has gained popularity as a teaching method because it emphasizes the role of Division as an operation which partitions a quantity into equal groups, and it also clearly shows the close link between Multiplication and Division.

Summary
This particular chapter has been structured to help bring some clarity to both the recommended progression and the new methods for teaching multiplication and division. Here are a few ways a parent can advocate for quality instruction of multiplication and division in grades 3-5:

1. Remember that, the new methods are only as useful as they are understood. Partial Products Multiplication should *not* be taught symbolically until students have been shown the Box Method, and the Box Method should *not* be practiced until teachers show the clear connection it has to finding area. Otherwise, we will simply teach students to perform operations with the same lack of clarity and with the same overfocus on memorization, not understanding, that we have been imparting for decades. The use of new methods does not automatically indicate better teaching.
2. This chapter gave special attention to ways by which we can correctly define multiplication and division. It is worth giving these definitions a second look, since the way that we view a concept strongly impacts how we teach it to our children.

When we teach from *incorrect* ideas about multiplication and division (such as simply reteaching memorized phrases like "carry the one" or "always put a zero in the second row") will not give students the kind of understanding necessary for long-term success. On the contrary, when we teach from good, clear, *correct* ideas about a concept, all of our teaching will make more sense and be easier to process for students.

3. If the *traditional* algorithms for multi-digit multiplication and long division are taught to students, it should be *after* they master the symbolic methods for Partial Products and Partial Quotients. These two techniques are the necessary stepping stones for making sense of the traditional algorithms.

For more specific details regarding the Common Core's Standards for introducing and teaching multiplication and division, see the information provided by the Common Core State Standards Initiative (2015b) on their website under the section headings for "Operations & Algebraic Thinking" and "Number and Operations in Base Ten".

See the Math in action!
Check out the companion videos for *Chapter 7* at www.commoncoremath101.com.

Chapter 8
Fractions

Fractions have long had a reputation for being disliked and misunderstood in math classrooms. Thus, it is not surprising that the CCSS-M have focused on strengthening the conceptual aspect of teaching fractions and now introduces the most basic fractional vocabulary as early as first grade (Common Core State Standards Initiative, 2015b, Grade 1: Geometry section). Some of this intentional structuring (and restructuring) of fraction education has popularized language and methods in the classroom that may seem unfamiliar to today's parents. These are the topics that I will explain in more detail throughout this section. However, if your student is struggling with fractions because of the gap in learning introduced by a sudden change to Common Core Standards without an early elementary background in CCSS-M fraction topics, please check out the additional electronic resources we have available on *www.commoncoremath101.com* and *www.mathstream.tv*. This concern has been especially vocalized by parents and teachers of fourth grade students, presumably because this is the age when students are expected to begin doing rather high level work with fractions. If their foundation has not been set before this time, the gaps in their understanding can cause major frustration for students, teachers, and parents.

The Value of the Number Line
After initial introduction using the more traditional methods of partitioned shapes and fraction words (like quarter, third, half, etc) to develop basic fraction knowledge, teachers are now focusing on the Number Line as an important foundation for understanding the relative size and value of different fractions. Consider this number line as we continue to discuss its application to fraction learning:

0   1

Students can use this number line to:

1) ...learn how to place various fraction values in their proper general location relative to 0 and 1.

Example 1A:

Place $\frac{1}{2}, \frac{1}{3}, \frac{1}{4}, \frac{1}{6}, \frac{2}{3}, \frac{7}{8},$ *and* $\frac{3}{4}$ *on the Number Line.*

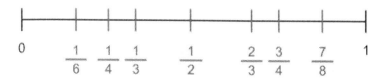

2) ...compare fractions to find which is larger and which is smaller by comparing their relative positions on the number line. This is called **Fraction Comparison to a Benchmark**. The three most common benchmarks that students can use to compare the relative sizes of fractions are: one-half, zero, and one.

Example 1B: *Use the number line to compare 11/24 and 3/5.*

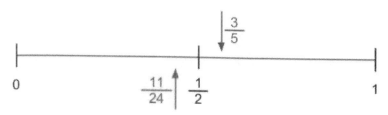

Using one-half as a benchmark, a student knows that 11/24 must be less than half, since 12/24 equals one-half. Similarly, 3/5 must be greater than half, since we would need 2.5/5 to make one-half or 3/6. Students know that 3/5 is greater than either of these quantities.

Therefore, 3/5 is greater than 11/24.

Example 1C: *Use the number line to compare 1/3 and 2/13.*

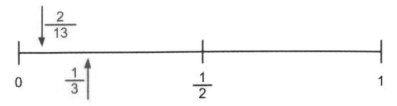

Using zero as a benchmark, a student knows that 2/13 is closer to zero than 1/3.
Therefore, 2/13 is less than 1/3.

Example 1D: *Use the number line to compare 26/27 and 5/6.*

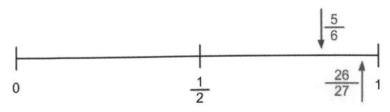

Using one as a benchmark, a student knows that 26/27 is closer to one than 5/6.
Therefore, 26/27 is greater than 5/6.

Using Partitioned Shapes for Fraction Addition and Subtraction

To help students understand the literal meaning of fraction addition and subtraction, introductory teaching of these topics makes use of a variety of visual supports. Consider the following example:

<u>Example 2A</u>

Shade the appropriate portion of the following circles to find this sum: $2\frac{5}{8} + 3\frac{7}{8}.$

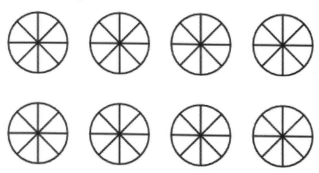

Step 1: Shade the whole quantities of both addends with different shades.

(In this case, the whole numbers are 2 and 3.)

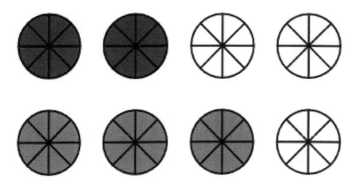

Step 2: Shade the fraction "parts" with their corresponding colors.

(In this case, we need 5 dark-shaded eighths and 7 light-shaded eighths.)

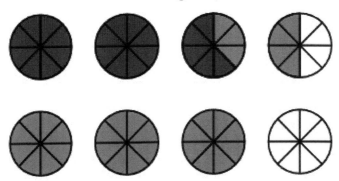

Step 3: Count the "Wholes" and "Parts" to find the sum.

There is a total of 6 "whole" circles that are shaded, and there is an additional $\frac{4}{8}$ or $\frac{1}{2}$ "part" of a circle shaded.

Thus, the solution to our original question is:

$$2\frac{5}{8} + 3\frac{7}{8} = 6\frac{1}{2}.$$

This same visual model can also be used to help students understand subtraction with fractions. Consider the following example:

<u>Example 2B:</u> Use the circle models to find the difference:

<u>Step 1:</u> Shade the initial quantity of $3\frac{1}{8}$.

<u>Step 2:</u> Mark or place an "X" on the quantity being "taken away", in this case, $2\frac{5}{8}$.

<u>Step 3</u>: Calculate the remaining quantity of "Wholes" and "Parts" to find the solution.

There are no "whole" circles remaining and only 4 eighths "Parts" that have not been marked. This remaining quantity can also be called 1 half. Therefore, our solution is:
$$3\tfrac{1}{8} - 2\tfrac{5}{8} = \tfrac{4}{8} = \tfrac{1}{2}.$$

Using this visual model, students are able to more intuitively grasp the ideas of regrouping and subtracting with fractional pieces. If a model had not been utilized, students would have been left to attempt to subtract ⅝ from ⅛, wondering how to get the extra "parts" they needed to complete the "take-away" process. When students eventually learn how to subtract using only symbols, the process of regrouping the question from $3\tfrac{1}{8} - 2\tfrac{5}{8}$ to $2\tfrac{9}{8} - 2\tfrac{5}{8}$ should feel more intuitive to them.

Visual Strategies for Multiplying Fractions and Whole Numbers

In order to utilize visual models to support Fraction Multiplication, it is important to review the definition of multiplication and view it from the perspective of fractions. If 2×4 means "2 groups of 4", and 1×4 means "1 group of four", then $\tfrac{1}{4} \times 4$ means "one-fourth of a group of 4". Similarly, and because of the commutative property of multiplication (aka, because a×b is the same as b×a), we can also think of $\tfrac{1}{4} \times 4$ as "four groups of one-fourth". Let us consider what this might look like using a visual model.

Example 3A

Model $\frac{1}{4} \times 4$ *as "one-fourth of a group of 4".*

Step 1: Draw an area that represents a "group of 4".

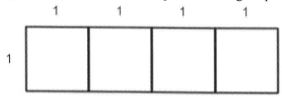

Step 2: Partition this area to show "one-fourth" of the group.

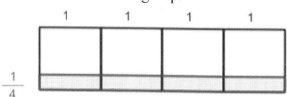

Step 3: Use the picture to decide what "one-fourth of a group of 4" equals.

Within each square, we have shaded an area equivalent to one-fourth.

We have four of these "one-fourths" shaded, and we know

$$\frac{1}{4} + \frac{1}{4} + \frac{1}{4} + \frac{1}{4} = \frac{4}{4} = 1$$.

Therefore, $\frac{1}{4} \times 4 = 1$.

Example 3B

Model $\frac{1}{4} \times 4$ as "4 groups of one-fourth".

Step 1: Draw the quantity "one-fourth".

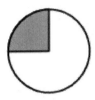

Step 2: Show "four groups" of this quantity.

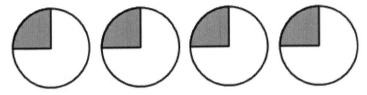

Step 3: Use the picture to decide what "4 groups of one-fourth" equals.

Within each circle, we have shaded an area equivalent to one-fourth.

We have four of these "one-fourths" shaded, and we know

$$\frac{1}{4} + \frac{1}{4} + \frac{1}{4} + \frac{1}{4} = \frac{4}{4} = 1.$$

Therefore, $\frac{1}{4} \times 4 = 1$.

To solidify the potential for this kind of model, let us consider one more example: $\frac{3}{5} \times 5$. Let us consider this multiplication sentence as "5 groups of $\frac{3}{5}$", or similarly, as "$\frac{3}{5}$ of 5 shapes".

Example 3C

Directions: Model $\frac{3}{5} \times 5$ and solve.

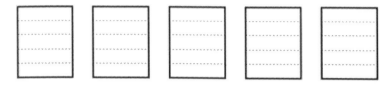

Solution to Example 3C

After identifying $\frac{3}{5}$ of each rectangle, we now have a total of $\frac{15}{5}$ shaded.
Thus, we find that $\frac{3}{5} \times 5 = \frac{15}{5} = 3$.

This visual model of fraction multiplication works for both whole number and mixed number solutions. (For example, $\frac{3}{5} \times 5$ yielded a whole number solution of "3", while $\frac{3}{5} \times 6$ would yield a mixed number solution of "$\frac{18}{5}$" or "$3\frac{3}{5}$", but the solution strategy of drawing and shading shapes would be the same for both multiplication sentences.)

Number Line Method for Multiplying by a Fraction
Using the same definition of fraction multiplication described in the previous section, let us consider how the **Number Line** can be used as an additional model and teaching tool. Let us consider $\frac{1}{4} \times 3$ specifically as "one-fourth of the distance to 3" or "one-fourth of the length 3".

<u>Example 4A</u>
Directions: Model $\frac{1}{4} \times 3$ on the number line below, and solve.

Step 1: The multiplication sentence indicates that we are breaking this length into "fourths", so we must partition each unit of the number line into fourths to complete our calculation.

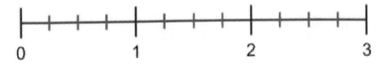

150

<u>Step 2:</u> Notice that there are now 12 steps to get from zero to three on this number line.
Find one-fourth of that length.

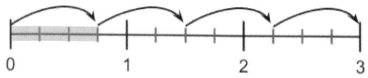

Using our number line, we see that "one-fourth of the length 3" is a small section of size "$\frac{3}{4}$".

Thus, the solution to our question is: $\frac{1}{4} \times 3 = \frac{3}{4}$.

Note that, as is true with any teaching model, the purpose of these learning strategies is to build conceptual understanding for the student. Eventually, it will become necessary that they learn and utilize more efficient methods for solving this type of problem. However, without a conceptual understanding of fraction multiplication, students frequently become confused by multiplication that yields unexpectedly small answers and thus become convinced that they are doing their work incorrectly.

Let us consider one more example before continuing:

Example 4B

Directions: Model $\frac{3}{5} \times 6$ on the number line below, and solve.

Solution to Example 4B

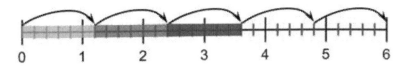

After dividing each interval into fifths (because we are multiplying by fifths),

we are able to find that 1/5 of the distance between zero and six is $1\frac{1}{5}$.

Therefore, 3/5 of the distance between zero and six is

$$1\frac{1}{5} + 1\frac{1}{5} + 1\frac{1}{5} = 3\frac{3}{5}. \text{ So, } \frac{3}{5} \times 6 = 3\frac{3}{5}.$$

Visual Strategies for Multiplying Two Fractions

If multiplying a whole number by a fraction means finding the fractional portion of an original *whole number* amount, then multiplying a fraction by another fraction means finding the fraction portion of an original *fraction* amount. Consider the following example:

Example 5A

Directions: Model the multiplication statement $\frac{1}{4} \times \frac{2}{3}$ *and solve.*

<u>Step 1</u>: Model the quantity $\frac{2}{3}$ by shading the appropriate region of a shape.

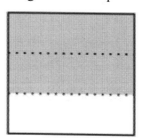

We have chosen a rectangle to represent one "whole" quantity, and we have shaded exactly two-thirds of it (partitioning it into thirds with horizontal lines).

Step 2: Find and Shade $\frac{1}{4}$ of the first shaded region.

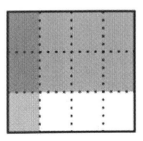

We originally divided the rectangle into Thirds using horizontal lines. Now, if we divide the rectangle into Fourths, using vertical lines, we can easily shade one-fourth of the rectangle using these lines as guides, simultaneously creating a Double-Shaded region which represents "one fourth of the original shaded region".

Note that the double shaded region mathematically reflects "one-fourth of the quantity two-thirds", or alternatively, it can also represent "two-thirds of the quantity one-fourth".

Step 3: Use the model to find the solution.

We want to know what "one-fourth of the quantity two thirds" (or $\frac{1}{4} \times \frac{2}{3}$) is equal to. Looking at our rectangle model, we see that the Purple Double-Shaded region is equivalent to the amount we are looking for. Using the vertical and horizontal dividing lines, it is apparent that we have divided the original rectangle into 12 equal pieces. Two of those 12 pieces are Double-Shaded.

Therefore, $\frac{1}{4} \times \frac{2}{3}$ is equal to $\frac{2}{12}$, or more simply, $\frac{1}{6}$.

For the sake of being thorough, consider this more simplified Example of Fraction Multiplication modeling which shows only the solution to $\frac{4}{5} \times \frac{1}{2}$:

Example 5B

Directions: Model the multiplication statement $\frac{4}{5} \times \frac{1}{2}$, and find the solution.

| Quantity: 1 | Horizontally Shade:
1/2 of the whole | Vertically Shade:
4/5 of the whole |

Double-Shaded: 4/5 of 1/2

Using the model, we find that four-fifths of the quantity one-half is $\frac{4}{10}$ or, more simply, $\frac{2}{5}$.

Division Involving Unit Fractions

In Fifth Grade, students must also consider the foundation of division involving fractions. First they must consider what it means to divide a unit fraction (a fraction whose top number, the numerator, is 1; Examples: 1/2, 1/3, 1/5, etc.) by a whole number. Secondly, they must consider what it means to divide a whole number by a unit fraction.

As a foundation for this topic, let us first recall the definition of division, which is: the process of partitioning a set of objects into a given number of equal groups and finding the amount in each group, or alternatively, it is the process of partitioning a set of objects into groups of a certain number and then finding the total number of groups. For instance, we can say that $8 \div 2$ means that we must take a set of 8 objects and divide them into 2 equal groups and find the amount in each group (Solution: 4 in each group), or we can say instead that $8 \div 2$ means that we must decide how many groups of 2 we can make from 8 objects (Solution: 4 groups of two).

The second definition for division is the easiest to apply to fractions. Let us consider a model that uses this definition as it applies to the division statement $8 \div \frac{1}{2}$.

Example 6A

*Directions: Model the Division Statement $8 \div \frac{1}{2}$ as the partitioning of the quantity "8" into equal groups of size ½, then solve. (Model Recommendation: **Tape Diagram**)*

Possible Solution to Example 6A
<u>Step 1</u>: Use a Tape Diagram to Model the quantity "8".
<u>Step 2</u>: Break 8 into groups of size ½.

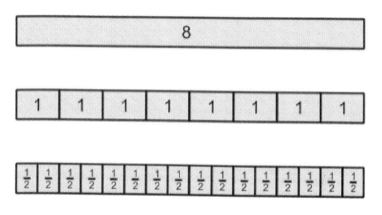

<u>Step 3</u>: Solve by finding the number of equal sized groups.
The Tape Diagram shows that there are 16 groups of one-half that fit in the quantity eight.

Therefore, $8 \div \frac{1}{2} = 16$.

This model also helps students to solidify their knowledge of the relationship between multiplication and division.

Here we find that $8 \div \frac{1}{2} = 16$ makes sense, since we also know that $16 \times \frac{1}{2} = 8$. This is the foundation for teaching fifth grade students how to divide whole numbers by unit fractions.

As previously discussed, fifth grade students must also discuss division of unit fractions by whole numbers. For

instance, we can consider the division statement: $\frac{1}{2} \div 8$.
The best model for this kind of problem is based on the first definition of division: the process of partitioning a set of objects into a given number of equal groups and finding the amount in each group.

Example 6B

Directions: Model the Division Statement $\frac{1}{2} \div 8$ as the quantity $\frac{1}{2}$ partitioned into 8 equal groups. Then find the solution by determining the size of each group.

Possible Solution to Example 6B

Step 1: Model the quantity of $\frac{1}{2}$.

Step 2: Divide that quantity into 8 equal groups.

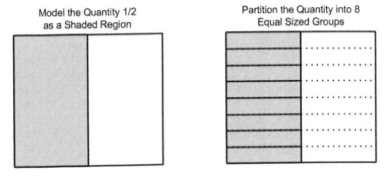

Model the Quantity 1/2 as a Shaded Region

Partition the Quantity into 8 Equal Sized Groups

Step 3: Find the solution by determining the size of the groups.

Recalling that the original shaded region was only Half, we know that our groups must be even smaller in size than a *half. Using the Model, we see that each group is of size $\frac{1}{16}$ (see model below).*

Find the Size of the Groups
by Comparing to the Whole

1/16	1/16
1/16	1/16
1/16	1/16
1/16	1/16
1/16	1/16
1/16	1/16
1/16	1/16
1/16	1/16

Thus, the solution to $\frac{1}{2} \div 8$ is $\frac{1}{16}$,

because $\frac{1}{2}$ partitioned into 8 equal groups yields groups of size $\frac{1}{16}$.

If Example 6B seems a bit abstract, consider the division statement $\frac{1}{2} \div 8$ as a real world situation. Suppose we had Half of a brownie pan still filled with dessert. If there are 8 people to divide the brownies among, what fraction of the brownie pan will each person eat? They will eat One-Sixteenth of the Pan if each person gets an equal share.

Summary

The main take-away from this review of current practices for teaching fractions is that picture models are critically important in helping students to make sense of fractions and fraction operations. In discussing the relationship

159

between working memory and long term memory during and following a learning episode, Sousa (2008) notes that the brain, after actively processing new information in working memory, will either choose to store the information for long term recall or decide to forget it completely. In regards to this, Sousa (2008) asks and answers a question that is critical for teachers to consider:

> What criteria does the working memory use to make that decision [to store or forget]? Information that has survival value is quickly stored along with strong emotional experiences. But in classrooms, where the survival and emotional elements are minimal or absent, other factors come into play. It seems that the working memory connects with the learner's past experiences and asks just two questions to determine whether an item is saved or rejected..."Does this make sense?"..."Does it have meaning?" (p. 55)

These are the two questions that teachers and parents should consider when seeking to impart long-term knowledge and understanding about fractions. Fractions are notorious for causing students major confusion and frustration. In fact, a group of researchers named Bezuk and Bieck (as cited in Chapin & Johnson, 2006) found that fractions were the single most problematic math topic for elementary and middle school aged students. That is a rather stunning statistic, given the wide range of mathematical material discussed during those years. As a means of addressing these concerns, the CCSS-M have highlighted these recommendations for better, more meaningful and memorable fraction learning:

1. Concrete, physical models and meaningful, pen and paper representations are critical in helping students to experiment with and understand fractions. There are two key reasons for the wide variety of visual teaching methods described in this chapter: firstly, different students understand and remember things differently, thus each student needs to experience a wide variety of options so that they can find the method that makes the most sense to them; and secondly, due to the abstract nature of fractions, it is important to make certain that the repetitive use of *one* model does not become overly generalized by students. For instance, if all of our pictures of fractions use images of circles and pies, students may forget or fail to realize that fractions can actually be depicted with *any* shape or even with a number-line.

2. Respected writer and math educator Marilyn Burns (2007) also advocates the importance of using real world situations to discern the areas of understanding and confusion regarding students' knowledge of fractions. However, contrary to the teacher-centric education that has become commonplace in our culture, she suggests that teachers give students a simple, symbolic fraction expression (such as $\frac{1}{4} + \frac{1}{3}$) and ask them to describe a real world situation that involves the given expression. Instead of giving students a word

problem and asking them to create an equation, Burns (2007) flips the problem around and asks the student to create a word-problem-like situation on their own. This activity will help empower the teacher or parent to listen for areas of comprehension and misunderstanding, so that they can more accurately bring meaning and correct conceptions of fractions.

3. Word Problems are also excellent tools to help explain fractional concepts that seem a bit strange when taken at face value. For instance, suppose your child is confused about why dividing 10 by ¼ gives us the rather large value of *40* as a solution. When students divide by whole numbers, their original value always gets smaller (for instance $10 \div 2 = 5$, so the original number, 10, becomes smaller when it is divided by the whole number 2). So why would division by the fraction ¼ give a result that is *larger* than the original number 10? A parent or teacher might help resolve this confusion by telling the following story: "Suppose there were 10 candy bars on the table, and I broke each candy bar into fourths. How many pieces of candy would be on the table when I was done?" This story illustrates a difficult concept in a meaningful way, and brings much more clarity to the situation than if the student was simply told, "Division by fractions usually make numbers larger. You should memorize that." That rule will most likely leave the student's working memory and be forgotten forever, or at least it will quickly disappear after the test is over.

4. Lastly, as was also true with the teaching of multiplication and division, the C-R-A method (Concrete-Representational-Abstract) is key to bringing a full, lasting understanding of fractional concepts. This means that concrete tools should be used to introduce new topics, and should progressively transition to the use of drawing representations and finally abstract, symbolic algorithms. The ultimate goal is that students will have a fluent understanding of symbolic methods for performing operations with fractions, but the patient process of transitioning from concrete to abstract is just as important as reaching that goal.

For more specific details regarding the Common Core's Standards for introducing fractions and operations with fractions, see the information provided by the Common Core State Standards Initiative (2015b) on their website under the section heading for "Geometry" and "Number & Operations--Fractions".

See the Math in action!
Check out the companion videos for *Chapter 8* at
www.commoncoremath101.com.

Chapter 9

Decimal
Numbers

Much of the homework I've seen for upper elementary study of decimal numbers is reminiscent of practice lessons that I myself was expected to complete as a young student. However, there are two key aspects that are worth discussing in regards to the Common Core Standards. Both of these, not surprisingly, are intended to help build a conceptual understanding and foundation for children's decimal and place value knowledge.

Writing Decimals in Expanded Form
Just as lower elementary students learned how to write large whole numbers in expanded form (see *Chapter 4:*

Understanding Place Value), upper elementary students must extend this knowledge to decimal values. In past decades of math education, we have often underemphasized the relationship between decimal numbers and their fractional equivalent. We have often read decimals like 0.67 as "point six seven" instead of its more accurate value of "67 hundredths", a clear reference to its fractional equivalent of $\frac{67}{100}$. This may seem to be a very trivial criticism, but consider the misconceptions that might occur in Example 1A if proper terminology is not emphasized.

Example 1
Directions: Decide which is greater, 0.67 *or* 0.7, and explain your reasoning.

Common **Incorrect** Solution to Example 1A
Possible Student Response: I think that 0.67 is greater than 0.7 since 67 is larger than 7.

Correct Solution to Example 1A
Using Proper Terminology: I know that 0.7 is greater than 0.67 because Seven-Tenths
(or 70-Hundredths) is more than 67-Hundredths.

When asking elementary students to identify the larger value, many mistakenly say that 0.67 is greater than 0.7 because they misunderstand the fractional value of the "67" and the "7". If we teach students to read decimals correctly (for instance, as $\frac{67}{100}$ and $\frac{7}{10}$), we will be more likely to help them develop functional, long-term, decimal understanding. One of the tools we use for drawing this connection between decimals and fractions is **Expanded Form**.

Example 2
Directions: Write 3,248.715 in Expanded Form.

Solution to Example 2

$$3(1000) + 2(100) + 4(10) + 8(1) + 7(\frac{1}{10}) + 1(\frac{1}{100}) + 5(\frac{1}{1000})$$

Note in Example 2 that the expression, if input into a calculator, would yield the original value of 3,248.715. However, the rather spread-out Expanded Form forces students to consider the relative fractional equivalent of each digit, instead of viewing all digits as having equal worth, a very easy and common mistake for elementary students to make.

In order for these fraction values to hold meaning for students, it is also important that they experiment with literal models of wholes, tenths, hundredths, etc. This is the second portion of decimal instruction that we should discuss in consideration of the conceptually rich math expectations of the Common Core.

Modeling Decimal Values

In any math classroom that is seeking to teach decimal knowledge through conceptual models, students are likely to be given math-work in which they will be asked to either identify or represent a decimal quantity (or its fractional equivalent) from a physical model or drawing. Consider the following examples of potential questions.

Example 3A

Directions: Consider the pictured value for "1", and then decide what the unidentified quantity must represent in decimal and fraction form.

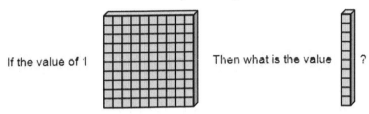

If the value of 1   Then what is the value   ?

Solution to Example 3A

In comparing the two quantities, we notice that we could fit 10 of the stick-blocks into the given "1" block. This means that the value of the unknown quantity is $\frac{1}{10}$ of 1, or simply:

$\frac{1}{10}$ (as a fraction) or 0.1 (as a decimal).

Example 3B

Directions: Consider the pictured value for "1", and then decide what the unidentified quantity must represent in decimal and fraction form.

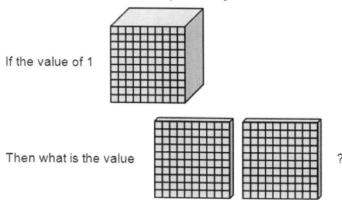

If the value of 1

Then what is the value   ?

Solution to Example 3B

In comparing the two quantities, we notice that we could fit 10 of the flat blocks into the given "1" cube. This means that the unknown quantity is made up of two blocks that are each worth the $\frac{1}{10}$ the value of 1, or simply: $\frac{1}{10} + \frac{1}{10} = \frac{2}{10}$ (as a fraction) or $0.1 + 0.1 = 0.2$ (as a decimal).

Example 3C

Directions: Consider the pictured value for "1", and then decide what the unidentified quantity must represent in decimal and fraction form.

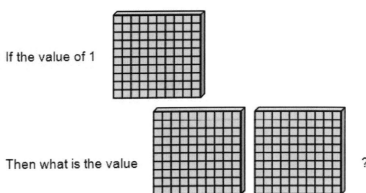

If the value of 1

Then what is the value   ?

Solution to Example 3B

In comparing the two quantities, we notice that the second quantity is simply twice the given value of "1". Therefore, the unknown value is $1 + 1 = 2$.

Directions: Consider the pictured value for "1", and then decide what the unidentified quantity must represent in decimal and fraction form.

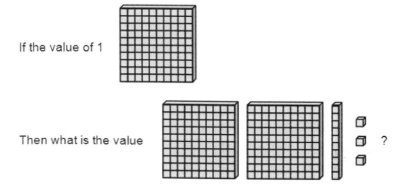

If the value of 1

Then what is the value   ?

Solution to Example 3D

Since the value of 1 is a flat block, the stick block must have a value of $\frac{1}{10}$ and the small cubes must each have a value of $\frac{1}{100}$. Therefore, the total unknown value must be

$$1 + 1 + \frac{1}{10} + \frac{1}{100} + \frac{1}{100} + \frac{1}{100} = 2 + \frac{1}{10} + \frac{3}{100} = 2 + \frac{10}{100} + \frac{3}{100} = 2\frac{13}{100}$$

(as a fraction)

or 2.13 (as a decimal).

Example 3E

Directions: Consider the pictured value for "1", and then decide what the unidentified quantity must represent in decimal and fraction form.

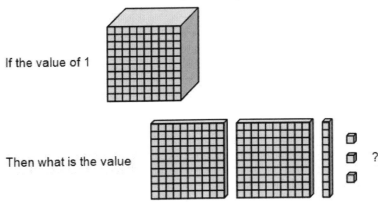

If the value of 1

Then what is the value ?

Solution to Example 3E

Since the value of 1 is a large cube, the flat blocks must each have a value of $\frac{1}{10}$, the stick blocks must each have a value of $\frac{1}{100}$, and the small cubes must each have a value of $\frac{1}{1000}$. Therefore, the total unknown value must be

$$\frac{1}{10} + \frac{1}{10} + \frac{1}{100} + \frac{1}{1000} + \frac{1}{1000} + \frac{1}{1000} = \frac{2}{10} + \frac{1}{100} + \frac{3}{1000} =$$

$$= \frac{200}{1000} + \frac{10}{1000} + \frac{3}{1000} = \frac{213}{1000}$$

(as a fraction) or 0.213 (as a decimal).

Summary

In many ways, decimal knowledge is an extension of fractional knowledge. Thus, the recommendations listed in the previous chapter also apply to this material as well. The most important two recommendations that are unique to decimals are the following:

1. Decimals should be named by their proper names to build fractional comparisons. For instance, the number 0.45 should be read as "45 hundredths" not as "point four five", since the mention of "hundredths" relates 0.45 to the fraction $\frac{45}{100}$ while the name "point four five" is abstract and relates very little mathematical meaning.

2. The visual comparison models in this section between *wholes* (quantity 1) and *parts* (decimal value) is the second important part of teaching decimal knowledge. The models used in Examples 3A to 3E utilize Base Ten Blocks to make the whole to part comparisons. If this is an exercise that you feel comfortable doing at home, you can use the free printables available on the internet (search: Base Ten Block Printables) to create your own exercises. Practice with these physical objects will provide an excellent foundation in decimal to fractional comparisons, proper decimal naming, and even a link for proper understanding of how to write decimals in expanded form.

For more specific details regarding the Common Core's Standards for introducing decimals in Grade 5, see the information provided by the Common Core State Standards Initiative (2015b) on their website under the section heading for Number & Operations in Base Ten" and "Number & Operations--Fractions".

See the Math in action!

Check out the companion videos for *Chapter 9* at
www.commoncoremath101.com.

In Closing

Conceptual
Understanding
is Key

At each level of math education, one key transition is common for all students: their work is being structured to build conceptual understanding, not simple memorization, as the foundation for all topics. This focus on conceptual understanding should never indicate that memorization is discouraged or absent from classroom interactions. Instead, memorization of mathematical ideas should become easier, and be more long lasting than they have been for past generations of students.

The Common Core State Standards for Mathematics have not been implemented as an attempt to advocate for "new math", but instead, we now have a group of standards which have set an expectation that teachers nationwide will begin to present "old math" in a more effective manner. As is always the case in educational shifts, there will be teachers who implement the new structure well, and there will be teachers who implement the new structure poorly. Hopefully, this book will give you enough information to advocate for your child at home and in the classroom, not to fight against the current methods, but rather to see them implemented in a worthy and helpful way. If you find that you still have questions, make sure to check out our other resources at *www.commoncoremath.com* and *www.mathstream.tv*.

Was this book helpful to you? We value your feedback. Please rate us on Amazon!

About the Author

Christen Nine has a Bachelors of Science in Mathematics and a Masters of Education in Moderate Disabilities. She is a certified Secondary Mathematics Teacher through the state of Massachusetts. She has taught high school math, both in the classroom and online, and currently serves on the board of directors for Christian Educators Academy, a private online school. Her combined passions for bringing meaningful, continuity to math education across all grade levels, for making math accessible and understandable to all students, and for seeing the Common Core State Standards for Mathematics implemented in a valuable and worthy manner, have been the key motivators behind this project.

References

Burns, M. (2007). *About teaching mathematics: A K-8 resource (3rd ed.). Sausalito, CA: Math Solutions.*

Chapin, S. H., & Johnson, A. (2006). *Math matters (2nd ed.).* Sausalito, CA: Math Solutions.

Common Core State Standards Initiative (2015a, Spring). *Grade 1: Operations & Algebraic Thinking.* Retrieved from http://www.corestandards.org/Math/Content/1/OA/

Common Core State Standards Initiative (2015b, Spring). *Mathematics Standards.* Retrieved from http://www.corestandards.org/Math/

Common Core State Standards Initiative (2015c, Spring). *Mathematics Glossary: Table 1.* Retrieved from http://www.corestandards.org/Math/Content/mathematics-glossary/Table-1/

Common Core State Standards Initiative (2015d, Spring). *Standards for Mathematical Practice.* Retrieved from http://www.corestandards.org/Math/Practice/

Sousa, D. A. (2008). *How the brain learns mathematics.* Thousand Oaks, CA: Corwin Press, A Sage Publications Company.

Van de Walle, J. A., Karp, K. S., & Bay-Williams, J. M. (2013). *Elementary and middle school mathematics: Teaching developmentally (Professional Development Ed.).* USA: Pearson Education.

Glossary

Adding On, 64

Area Model, 118
  of multiplication, 119

Array
  with multiplication, 115

Arrays, 37

Bar Graph, 108

Base Ten Blocks, 49
  addition & subtraction, 73

Borrowing, 83

Box Method
  (or Area Model), 125

Carry the One, 77

Common Core State Standards
  Initiative Website, 29

Composing 10, 76

Concrete-Representational-
  Abstract, 94
  with fractions, 163

Counting Back, 66

Counting On, 65

Decimal Values
  modeling, 167

Decomposing Numbers, 47
  with base ten blocks, 84

Division
  definition, 131

Division Involving Unit
  Fractions, 155

Expanded Form, 55
  with partial sums, 91
  with decimal numbers, 167

Fraction Addition and
  Subtraction, 143

Fraction Comparison to a
  Benchmark, 141

Fraction Multiplication, 146

Making 10, 37
  addition with ten frames, 71
  composing 10 with base ten
    blocks, 76
  subtraction with ten frames,
    73

Multiplication
  definition, 114

Multiplying Two Fractions,
  152

Number Line, 39
  addition & subtraction, 64
  fraction multiplication, 150
  with fractions, 140

Partial Differences, 92

Partial Products, 126

Partial Quotients, 134

Partial Sums, 91

Partition, 38

Partitioned Shapes
  with fractions, 143

Picture Graph, 104

Regrouping, 78

Standards for Mathematical
  Practice, 12

Subitizing, 34

Tape Diagram, 48, 62
  fraction division, 156

Ten Frame, 35

Ten Frames
  (Addition & Subtraction),
    68

Tree Diagram, 48

Made in the USA
Columbia, SC
24 October 2018